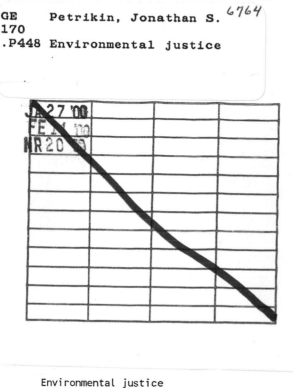

# ENVIRONMENTAL JUSTICE

Other Books in the At Issue Series:

# ENVIRONMENTAL JUSTICE

David Bender, *Publisher*
Bruno Leone, *Executive Editor*

Katie de Koster, *Managing Editor*
Scott Barbour, *Series Editor*

Jonathan S. Petrikin, *Book Editor*

AT ISSUE

An Opposing Viewpoints Series®

Greenhaven Press, Inc.
San Diego, California

Library of Congress Cataloging-in-Publication Data

At issue: environmental justice / book editor, Jonathan Petrikin.
        p.    cm. — (At issue series) (Opposing viewpoint series)
    Includes bibliographical references and index.
    ISBN 1-56510-264-9  (pbk.) — ISBN 1-56510-297-5 (lib.).
    1.  Environmental policy—United States. 2. Hazardous waste
sites—United States. 3. Afro-Americans—Politics and government.
4. Racism—United States. [1. Environmental policy. 2. Discrimination.]
I. Petrikin, Jonathan S., 1963-   . II. Series. III. Opposing viewpoints
series (unnumbered).
GE170.A8   1995                                              94-28350
363.7′00973—dc20                                                 CIP
                                                                 AC

© 1995 by Greenhaven Press, Inc., PO Box 289009,
San Diego, CA 92198-9009

Printed in the U.S.A.

# Table of Contents

# Introduction

Altgeld Gardens is an African-American community in the south side of Chicago. Built atop a 19th-century landfill and surrounded by eleven polluting facilities, ranging from sewage treatment plants to incinerators and oil refineries, Altgeld Gardens is considered by some to be a classic example of what has been termed "environmental racism"—the siting of a disproportionate number of the nation's industrial and waste facilities in or near minority residential areas. "Cancer Alley" is another often-cited example: Lining an 80-mile strip of the lower Mississippi River are the more than 100 oil refineries and petrochemical plants that have so polluted the environment that several of the local communities of color—many of them historic—are being abandoned. According to the U.S. Environmental Protection Agency (EPA), an "unusually high incidence of cancer, asthma, hypertension, strokes, and other illnesses" plague the citizens who remain in the region.

Those who see in these beleaguered areas the work of environmental racism assert that communities of color are unfairly targeted as sites for polluting facilities because, unlike white neighborhoods, they lack the political representation and economic resources necessary to oppose powerful corporations. Beginning in the 1980s, members of several minority and poor communities began organizing to fight against what they perceived as environmental racism in their neighborhoods and nationwide. In 1989 residents of Cancer Alley organized the first Great Louisiana Toxic March to bring attention to their living conditions. Two years later 300 delegates from grassroots environmental justice groups across the United States—including an Altgeld Gardens representative—convened the First National People of Color Environmental Leadership Summit in Washington, D.C., where they networked and drafted a manifesto. By this time, the environmental justice movement had been reinforced academically with the publication of several demographic studies asserting not only the existence of environmental racism but also the federal government's complicity, through inaction, in that racism.

Others contend, however, that market forces, not racist practices, determine the siting of polluting facilities. "Environmental hazards are likely to be placed in any community that . . . is willing to accept risks because they create jobs or generate taxes," New York Law School professor David Schoenbrod explains. Moreover, Schoenbrod asserts, in many cases—such as Altgeld Gardens, which was built atop a landfill—"the environmental hazards did not come to minority neighborhoods, but rather the minority populations came to the hazards."

Often cited in support of this view is a 1994 study by New York University associate law professor Vicki Been, who examined and expanded on two earlier studies that had found evidence of environmental racism. Been concluded that it was only "after the sitings [of polluting industries that] the levels of poverty and percentages of African-Americans in the

7

host neighborhoods increased." There are two reasons for this, she argues. First, those who can afford to leave the area once a facility is sited tend to do so, leaving behind those who cannot afford to move or who are prevented from relocating by the racial discrimination they encounter in other housing markets. Second, since the property values of the host community decline after the siting, it is the poor and minorities who tend to move there to take advantage of the cheaper housing. "Even if siting processes can be improved," Been concludes, "market forces are likely to create a pattern in which [polluting facilities] become surrounded by people of color or the poor, and consequently come to impose a disproportionate burden on [them]."

Environmental justice advocates respond that Been's focus on "market forces" is an attempt to derail their movement by transforming an issue of social justice into an economic matter. Robert Bullard, a Clark Atlanta University, sociology professor who was one of the first to research and publish allegations of environmental racism, argues that Been's and similar studies were undertaken in order to stop incipient—and, for businesses, expensive—federal efforts to legislate environmental justice. The most prominent of these efforts, Bullard relates, is President Bill Clinton's 1994 executive order directing each federal agency to make "environmental justice part of its mission" by ensuring that its operations do not have a disproportionately high and adverse environmental effect on poor and minority communities. The EPA had already begun to respond to the environmental justice issue in 1992, Bullard explains, with its creation of the Office of Environmental Justice—which coordinates federal efforts to ensure environmental equity—and with the reformulation of EPA qualifications for environmental cleanup to consider the effects of multiple types of pollution that affect communities like Altgeld Gardens. In addition to these initiatives, Bullard also advocates legislation that would ensure the collection of demographic information before the siting of any future industries and the prevention of any sitings in already disadvantaged communities. "It is not enough to demonstrate the existence of unjust and unfair conditions," he concludes; "the practices that cause the conditions must be made illegal."

But these solutions are based on the erroneous assumption that the current practices of siting noxious facilities are essentially social in nature, instead of the result of market forces, assert Christopher Boerner and Thomas Lambert in a study they conducted in 1994 for Washington University's Center for the Study of American Business. Agreeing with Been, the two contend that banning the development of polluting industries will not result in environmental justice. Rather, Boerner and Lambert say, "proposals to prohibit, limit, or discourage polluting facilities from locating in minority and low-income communities deny those areas the economic benefits associated with hosting industrial and waste plants." These benefits, which include jobs and revenue, the authors contend, "far outweigh the costs of hosting such facilities." Boerner and Lambert advocate an arrangement whereby citizens who suffer the costs of a polluting industry would receive financial compensation, through taxes or other means, from those who enjoy its benefits. The authors maintain that this policy would allow communities to weigh the risks and benefits of hosting polluting industries rather than having all opportunities denied them by intrusive legislation. They conclude that "inflexible siting and permitting policies which work to deny some individuals the opportunity to accept small risks and inconveniences in order to substantially better themselves economically are patently paternalistic and ultimately unjust."

David Schoenbrod argues that legislative initiatives to address environmental justice will also likely prove expensive and problematic to enforce. On the other hand, minority communities continue to demand remedies for what they perceive as environmental racism. Cheryl Johnson of Altgeld Gardens' People for Community Recovery argues that by failing to address their concerns, society is "saying we're expendable, we're not important." Whether racism or market forces determine the location of polluting industries and how environmental justice can be assured are among the topics discussed in *At Issue: Environmental Justice.*

# 1

# Demographic Studies Reveal a Pattern of Environmental Injustice

## Paul Mohai and Bunyan Bryant

*Paul Mohai and Bunyan Bryant are associate professors at the School of Natural Resources at the University of Michigan in Ann Arbor. Mohai and Bryant were the principal investigators for the University of Michigan's 1990 study of the distribution of waste facilities in the Detroit, Michigan, area and were organizers of the school's January 1990 Conference on Race and the Incidence of Environmental Hazards in Ann Arbor, Michigan. They also served on the National Advisory Committee of the First National People of Color Environmental Leadership Summit— the first convocation of the nation's grassroots environmental justice groups—held in October 1991 in Washington, D.C.*

Fifteen studies that evaluate the social distribution of pollution are compared, yielding demographic evidence that environmental hazards are distributed on the basis of race, and to a lesser extent poverty—a phenomenon dubbed by this and earlier studies "environmental racism." In five of the eight studies that assessed the relative importance of race and income, race was found to be a more significant factor than income in determining exposure to environmental hazard. This finding is echoed by the University of Michigan's 1990 Detroit Area Study, which correlates race and income with the distribution of hazardous waste sites in Detroit to find that a minority resident is about four times more likely than a white citizen to live within a mile of a waste site. The race factor is found not only to be independent of income but a stronger predictor of exposure to pollution—an inequity that requires "proactive government policies . . . to address this issue."

The United Church of Christ's (1987) report on the distribution of hazardous waste sites in this country has been very influential in raising public awareness about the disproportionate burden of pollution on minorities. This study is important because of its national scope and because of its strong and unequivocal findings regarding the distribution of com-

Chapter 13, "Environmental Racism: Reviewing the Evidence," of *Race and the Incidence of Environmental Hazards*, Bunyan Bryant and Paul Mohai, eds., 1992. Reprinted by permission of Westview Press, Boulder, Colorado.

mercial hazardous waste facilities. It found that the proportion of residents who are minorities in communities that have a commercial hazardous waste facility is about double the proportion of minorities in communities without such facilities. Where two or more such facilities are located, the proportion of residents who are minorities is more than triple. This study further demonstrated that race is the single best predictor of where commercial hazardous waste facilities are located, even when other socioeconomic characteristics of communities, such as average household income and average value of homes, are taken into account.

---

*Minority communities are at a disadvantage not only in terms of availability of resources but also because of underrepresentation on governing bodies.*

---

The United Church of Christ report concluded that it is "virtually impossible" that the nation's commercial hazardous waste facilities are distributed disproportionately in minority communities merely by chance, and that underlying factors related to race, therefore, in all likelihood play a role in the location of these facilities. Among others these factors include: 1) the availability of cheap land, often located in minority communities and neighborhoods (Asch and Seneca, 1978; Bullard and Wright, 1987; United Church of Christ, 1987); 2) the lack of local opposition to the facility, often resulting from minorities' lack of organization and political resources as well as their need for jobs (Bullard and Wright, 1987; United Church of Christ, 1987); and 3) the lack of mobility of minorities resulting from poverty and housing discrimination that traps them in neighborhoods where hazardous waste facilities are located (Bullard and Wright, 1987; United Church of Christ, 1987). The United Church of Christ report noted that these mechanisms and resulting inequitable outcomes represent institutionalized forms of racism. When the report was released, Dr. Benjamin F. Chavis, Jr., termed the racial biases in the location of commercial hazardous waste facilities as "environmental racism" (Lee, 1992).

The striking findings and the scope of the United Church of Christ study suggest that environmental racism is not confined to hazardous waste alone. A major objective of our investigation was, therefore, to document the existence of other studies which have used systematic data to examine the social distribution of pollution and to determine whether the evidence from these studies, taken together, demonstrates a consistent pattern of environmental racism.

A question that is often raised is whether the racial bias in the distribution of environmental hazards is simply a function of poverty (see, for example, Weisskopf, 1992). That is, rather than race per se, is it not poverty that affects the distribution of environmental hazards? And are not minorities disproportionately impacted simply because they are disproportionately poor?[1] Classical economic theory would predict that poverty plays a role (see Asch and Seneca, 1978, and Freeman, 1972). Because of limited income and wealth, poor people do not have the financial means to buy out of polluted neighborhoods and into environmentally more desirable ones. Also, land values tend to be cheaper in poor neighborhoods and are thus attractive to polluting industries that seek to

reduce the costs of doing business (United Church of Christ, 1987). However, housing discrimination further restricts the mobility of minorities
(Denton and Massey, 1988; Feagin and Feagin, 1978).[2] Also, because noxious sites are unwanted (the "NIMBY" syndrome) and because industries
tend to take the path of least resistance, communities with little political
clout are often targeted for such facilities (Bullard and Wright, 1987).
These communities tend to be where residents are unaware of the policy
decisions affecting them and are unorganized and lack resources for taking political action; such resources include time, money, contacts, knowledge of the political system, and others (Bullard, 1990; Mohai, 1985,
1990). Minority communities are at a disadvantage not only in terms of
availability of resources but also because of underrepresentation on governing bodies when location decisions are made (Bullard, 1983). Underrepresentation translates into limited access to policy makers and lack of
advocates for minority interests.

Taken together, these factors suggest that race has an additional impact on the distribution of environmental hazards, independent of income. A second major objective of our study, therefore, was to assess the
relative influence of income and race on the distribution of pollution. We
did so by examining the results of those empirical studies which have analyzed the distribution of environmental hazards by both income and
race. To our knowledge, this is the first time such a review and assessment
has been undertaken. We also provide new evidence from a multivariate
analysis of the distribution of commercial hazardous waste facilities in
the Detroit metropolitan area.

## Environmental racism: Evidence from existing studies

Table 1 contains a summary of 15 studies which provide systematic information about the social distribution of environmental hazards. In assessing the distribution of these hazards by income, the typical approach
has been to correlate the average or median household or family income
of the community (usually approximated by U.S. Census tracts or zip
code areas) with the degree of exposure to the hazard. In assessing the distribution of environmental hazards by race, the minority percentage of
the community has been typically employed. For example, after match-
ing the location of air quality monitoring sites with U.S. Census tracts,
Asch and Seneca (1978) correlated the median family incomes and minority percentages of the Census tracts with the mean annual air pollution levels of the tracts. Likewise, the United Church of Christ (1987)
matched the location of commercial hazardous waste facilities with zip
code areas, and correlated the mean household income, minority percentage, and other characteristics of these areas with the presence of one
or more commercial hazardous waste facilities.

A number of interesting and important facts emerge from an examination of Table 1. First, an inspection of the publication dates of these
studies reveals that information about environmental inequity has been
available for some time. Rather than being a recent discovery, documentation of environmental injustices stretches back two decades, almost to
Earth Day [1970]—an event viewed by many as a major turning point in
public awareness about environmental issues (Davies and Davies, 1975;
Fessler, 1990). Evidently, it has taken some time for public awareness to
catch up to the issues of environmental injustice.

**Table 1.** Studies Providing Systematic Empirical Evidence Regarding the Burden of Environmental Hazards by Income and Race

| Study | Hazard | Focus of Study | Distribution Inequitable by Income? | Distribution Inequitable by Race? | Income or Race More Important? |
|---|---|---|---|---|---|
| CEQ (1971) | Air Poll. | Urban Area | Yes | NA* | NA |
| Freeman (1972) | Air Poll. | Urban Areas | Yes | Yes | Race |
| Harrison (1975) | Air Poll. | Urban Areas | Yes | NA | NA |
| | Air Poll. | Nation | No | NA | NA |
| Kruvant (1975) | Air Poll. | Urban Area | Yes | Yes | Income |
| Zupan (1975) | Air Poll. | Urban Area | Yes | NA | NA |
| Burch (1976) | Air Poll. | Urban Area | Yes | No | Income |
| Berry et al. (1977) | Air Poll. | Urban Areas | Yes | Yes | NA |
| | Solid Waste | Urban Areas | Yes | Yes | NA |
| | Noise | Urban Areas | Yes | Yes | NA |
| | Pesticide Poisoning | Urban Areas | Yes | Yes | NA |
| | Rat Bite Risk | Urban Areas | Yes | Yes | NA |
| Handy (1977) | Air Poll. | Urban Area | Yes | NA | NA |
| Asch & Seneca (1978) | Air Poll. | Urban Areas | Yes | Yes | Income |
| Gianessi et al. (1979) | Air Poll. | Nation | No | Yes | Race |
| Bullard (1983) | Solid Waste | Urban Area | NA | Yes | NA |
| U.S. GAO (1983) | Haz. Waste | Southern Region | Yes | Yes | NA |
| United Church of Christ (1987) | Haz. Waste | Nation | Yes | Yes | Race |
| Gelobter (1987; 1992) | Air Poll. | Urban Areas | Yes | Yes | Race |
| | Air Poll. | Nation | No | Yes | Race |
| West et al. (1992) | Toxic Fish Consumption | State | No | Yes | Race |

\* NA = not applicable.

It is also interesting to note that most of the studies that have been conducted in this period have focused on the distribution of air pollution. Clearly, systematic studies of the social distribution of other types of environmental hazards, such as water pollution, pesticide exposure, asbestos exposure, and other hazards are needed. Also worth noting is that these studies vary considerably in terms of their scope—i.e., some studies have focused on single urban areas, such as Washington, DC, or Houston, others have focused on a collection of urban areas, while still others have been national in scope. This observation is important in that it reveals that the pattern of findings is not simply an artifact of the samples used. Regardless of the scope of the analyses, the findings point to a consistent pattern.

It is clear from examining the results in Table 1 that, regardless of the environmental hazard and regardless of the scope of the study, in nearly every case the distribution of pollution has been found to be inequitable by income. And with only one exception, the distribution of pollution has been found to be inequitable by race. Where the distribution of pollution has been analyzed by both income and race (and where it was possible to weigh the relative importance of each), in most cases race has been found to be more strongly related to the incidence of pollution.

The United Church of Christ (1987), Freeman (1972), Gelobter (1987, 1992), Gianessi, Peskin, and Wolff (1979), and West, Fly, Larkin, and Marans (1992) all found that race was more strongly related than class to the distribution of the environmental hazard under investigation. As mentioned previously, from a multivariate statistical analysis of nationwide data, the United Church of Christ found that the percentage of minority residents within a community (defined by zip code areas) was the single best predictor of where commercial hazardous waste facilities are located in the country—more so than other socioeconomic variables such as mean household income and mean value of owner-occupied homes.

Using an air pollution exposure index, Freeman (1972) found that low-income groups in three urban areas (Kansas City, St. Louis, and Washington, DC) were more greatly exposed to total suspended particulates and sulfates than upper-income groups. However, racial differences were found to be even more pronounced as minorities in each of the cities were found to be exposed to higher levels of both pollutants than the lowest income group examined (the "under $3,000" group).

---

*If you . . . are a minority resident, your chance of living within a mile of a hazardous waste facility is about four times greater than if you are white.*

---

Likewise using pollution exposure indices (one for total suspended particulates and another for combined concentrations of total suspended particulates, sulfates, sulfur dioxide, nitrogen oxides, ozone, and carbon monoxide), Gelobter (1987,1992) found similar results. However, unlike Freeman's study Gelobter's was national in scope. He conducted his analyses in two parts, one focused on the U.S. as a whole, incorporating both rural and urban areas, and a second focused on just urban areas. He found that over a 15-year period (from 1970 to 1984) minorities were consistently exposed to significantly more air pollution than whites. This finding was the same whether the analysis was focused on just the urban areas or on the country as a whole. Inequities in the distribution of air pollution by income were less clear. At the national level, exposure to total suspended particulates was found to be somewhat greater for upper income groups than for lower income groups (a probable result of the fact that both income and pollution tend to be simultaneously higher in urban areas than in rural ones). Within urban areas, however, exposure was found to be greater for those in the lower income categories, although differences by income categories tended to be small. When exposure to combined concentrations of air pollutants was examined, similar patterns were found, although this time lower income groups were found to be more greatly exposed at both national and urban levels of analyses. Nevertheless, as in Freeman's study, racial biases in exposure to pollution tended to be more stark; as in the earlier study, in all cases minorities were found to be more greatly exposed to pollution than the lowest income group examined ("under $3,000").

Gianessi, Peskin, and Wolff's (1979) study is the only other to have attempted a national level analysis of the distribution of air pollution by income and race. However, unlike Gelobter's study, rather than measuring exposure to physical concentrations of air pollution directly, they estimated dollar damage suffered from exposure to air pollution. Also, their estimates were based on EPA data taken for a single time period. Nevertheless, their results are very similar to Gelobter's. Like Gelobter, they found that air pollution damage is distributed progressively (i.e., upper rather than lower income groups suffer more damage) when the analysis is conducted at the national level (as before, this outcome is the probable result of incomes and pollution tending to be simultaneously higher in the more urbanized rather than rural areas of the country). However, when racial differences were examined, the inequities were found to be clear and striking: minorities were much more likely to suffer greater damage from air pollution than whites at all income levels.

Finally, West, Fly, Larkin, and Marans (1992) found from a state-wide survey of licensed fishermen in Michigan that on average minority fishermen and their families are likely to consume more fish (21.7 grams/person/day) than white fishermen and their families (17.9 grams/person/day). The purpose of their study was to assess the potential risk to these groups of ingesting toxic fish. Michigan's Rule 1057, which is designed to regulate the amount of discharge of toxic chemicals into state waters, is based on the assumption that the average consumption of fish in the state is 6.5 grams/person/day (West et al., 1992). Although minority fishermen and their families were found to consume more fish than white fishermen and their families, clearly both groups appear to be at risk based on this standard. Interestingly, West et al. did not find a significant relationship between income and the amount of fish consumed in either their bivariate analysis of income with consumption nor in their multivariate analysis where the simultaneous relationship of income and race with consumption was examined.

*Current environmental policies have allowed for separate societies differing in the quality of their respective environments.*

Only in 3 of the 8 studies where it was possible to weigh the relative importance of both race and income was income found to be more strongly related to the distribution of environmental hazards. In one of these studies, Kruvant (1975) superimposed Census tract data in the Washington, DC, area with air pollution zones. Using this method, he found that there tended to be a tighter fit between areas of high air pollution and high concentrations of the poor than there were between areas of high air pollution concentrations and blacks. Using a similar technique, Burch (1976) found that while there was a significant relationship between areas of high air pollution and high concentrations of the poor in the New Haven, CT, area, there was no significant relationship between concentrations of air pollution and blacks. Finally, Asch and

Seneca (1978) found that the correlations of the "nonwhite" percentages of Census tracts in Chicago, Cleveland, and Nashville with the mean annual levels of various air pollutants tended to be weaker than the correlations of the median family incomes of the Census tracts with pollutant levels; using cities within 23 states (rather than Census tracts within the 3 cities mentioned above) as the units of analysis, Asch and Seneca obtained similar results.

Although 2 additional studies found the distribution of environmental hazards to be inequitable by both income and race, it was not possible to assess conclusively which, if either, variable was more strongly related because of the methodological approaches employed in these studies. These include Berry et al.'s study (1977) of the distribution of air pollution, pesticide poisoning, noise, solid waste, and rat bite risks in 13 of the nation's major urban areas, and the U.S. General Accounting Office's study (1983) of the distribution of four major hazardous waste landfills located in the South.

In summary, review of the 15 studies which have examined the distribution of environmental hazards by income and race indicates both a class and racial bias. Furthermore, that the racial bias is not simply a function of poverty alone also appears to be born out by the data. All but one of the 11 studies which have examined the distribution of environmental hazards by race have found a significant bias. In addition, in 5 of the 8 studies where it was possible to assess the relative importance of race with income, racial biases have been found to be more significant. Noteworthy also is the fact that all 3 studies which have been national in scope and which have provided both income and race information have found race to be more importantly related to the distribution of environmental hazards than income. Taken together, these findings thus appear to support the assertion of those who have argued that race has an additional effect on the distribution of environmental hazards that is independent of class.

## Environmental racism: evidence from the Detroit Area Study

In order to provide greater clarity to the issue of environmental equity, we provide additional evidence from an analysis of the distribution of commercial hazardous waste facilities in the Detroit area. In so doing, special attention is given to the effects of race. A detailed multivariate statistical analysis is conducted in order to determine whether race has a relationship with the location of commercial hazardous waste facilities that is independent of income. The multivariate analysis is also used to weigh the relative strength of the relationship of race and income with the distribution of sites. There are only 2 other studies which have applied multivariate statistical techniques to assess the relative effects of race and income on exposure to environmental hazards: the United Church of Christ (1987) and West et al. (1992) studies. Both found race not only to have an independent relationship with the hazard but also found it to be more strongly related to the hazard than income.

Data used for this study are taken from the University of Michigan's 1990 Detroit Area Study (Mohai and Bryant, 1989). Information was obtained from face-to-face interviews of residents 18 years or older in Macomb, Oakland, and Wayne Counties, Michigan (the 3 counties surrounding the city of Detroit). Respondents were identified from households which were selected with equal probability using a stratified two-stage area probability sampling design. Because of the objectives of the study, an additional oversample was drawn of households within 1.5 miles of an existing or proposed commercial hazardous waste treatment or storage facility. Information about the location of the facilities in the Detroit area was obtained from the Michigan Department of Natural Resources. These included 14 existing facilities and 2 proposed.[3]

L. Kish (1949) selection tables were used to randomly select one respondent from the eligible persons in each of the households in the base (households not within 1.5 miles of a facility) and supplemental studies. Five hundred four and 289 interviews, respectively, in the two samples were conducted resulting in an overall study response rate of 69 percent.

For all analyses, cases were weighted by the number of eligible persons in the household. In those analyses where the oversample and base samples were pooled, cases were additionally weighted by a household sampling weight which compensates for the unequal probability of selection between the two samples.

Information about race and household income was obtained for all 793 respondents. The unweighted numbers of whites, blacks, and other nonwhites in the sample were 575, 180, and 38, respectively. For purposes of the analyses the 218 blacks and other nonwhites were combined into the category "minority."

The precise locations of the commercial hazardous waste facilities and the 289 respondents in the oversample were mapped. The distances between these respondents and one of the 16 facilities was measured to the nearest 0.1 mile.

Although our main objective was to assess racial biases in the distribution of commercial hazardous waste facilities within the 3 counties surrounding the city of Detroit, from a cursory analysis we observed a rather striking racial bias in the distribution of these facilities at the state level as well. Although there are 21 commercial hazardous waste facilities in the state of Michigan, 16 (76 percent) of them are located in the 3-county area. And of these 16, half (the 2 facilities that are proposed are included here) are located in the city of Detroit, proper. This is significant as U.S. Census Bureau data for the state of Michigan and demographic data collected from our Detroit area study indicate that the minority percentages for the state, 3-county area, and city are 16 percent, 21 percent, and 76 percent, respectively. Thus, commercial hazardous waste facilities in the state are clearly located disproportionately where minorities are most heavily concentrated.

Our next step was to conduct a detailed analysis of the distribution of commercial hazardous waste facilities within the 3-county metropolitan area, giving special attention to the relative effects of income and race. Using the demographic and socioeconomic information from the 504 residents in our base sample (those in the Detroit area who live more than 1.5 miles away from a commercial hazardous waste facility), we computed the percent who are minority residents as well as the percent who are living below the poverty line.[4] We did likewise with the oversample of 289 residents living within 1.5 miles of a facility. However, we further divided this latter sample into those living strictly within 1 mile of and those living between 1 mile and 1.5 miles from a facility.

*Figure 1.* **Percent of Detroit Area Residents Living Near a Commercial Hazardous Waste Facility Who Are Members of a Minority Group or Who Live Below the Poverty Line**

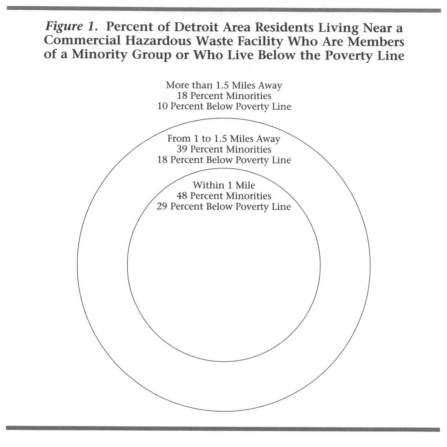

More than 1.5 Miles Away
18 Percent Minorities
10 Percent Below Poverty Line

From 1 to 1.5 Miles Away
39 Percent Minorities
18 Percent Below Poverty Line

Within 1 Mile
48 Percent Minorities
29 Percent Below Poverty Line

The diagram in Figure 1 indicates the percent of minorities and the percent of people living below the poverty line within fixed distances of a commercial hazardous waste facility. The percentages indicate a clear bias. Of those people living more than 1.5 miles from a commercial hazardous waste facility only 18 percent are minority residents. Of those people living within 1.5 miles but more than 1 mile away, 39 percent are minority. And of those residents living within 1 mile from the center of a facility, 48 percent are minority. A similar pattern exists when the percentage of people living below the poverty line are examined (see Figure 1). Chi-square tests indicate that these patterns are statistically significant at the .0000 level (see Table 2).

Analysis of our data indicates that only about 4 percent of the total population in the three-county area lives within 1 mile of a commercial hazardous waste facility. Broken down by racial groups, 3 percent of all whites and 11 percent of all minorities live within a mile of such a facility. Although these are small proportions for both groups, the biases are nevertheless clear. As the ratio of the two percentages indicate, if you are living in the 3-county area of Detroit and are a minority resident, your chance of living within a mile of a hazardous waste facility is about four times greater than if you are white.

We wanted to determine whether the above results were a function

**Table 2.** Percent of Detroit Area Residents Living Within Fixed Distances of a Commercial Hazardous Waste Facility Who Are Members of a Minority Group or Living Below the Poverty Line

| All Three-County Area Residents | White | Minority | Above Poverty Line | Below Poverty Line |
|---|---|---|---|---|
| > 1.5 miles away | 82 | 18 | 90 | 10 |
| 1–1.5 miles away | 61 | 39 | 82 | 18 |
| < 1 mile away | 52 | 48 | 71 | 29 |

Chi-square = 26.6328          Chi-square = 56.6610
d.f. = 2                      d.f. = 2
P = 0.0000                    P = 0.0000

| City of Detroit Residents | White | Minority | Above Poverty Line | Below Poverty Line |
|---|---|---|---|---|
| > 1.5 miles away | 25 | 76 | 66 | 34 |
| 1–1.5 miles away | 21 | 79 | 85 | 15 |
| < 1 mile away | 20 | 80 | 48 | 52 |

Chi-square = 0.4651           Chi-square = 11.3457
d.f. = 2                      d.f. = 2
P = 0.7925                    P = 0.0034

| Suburban Residents | White | Minority | Above Poverty Line | Below Poverty Line |
|---|---|---|---|---|
| > 1.5 miles away | 93 | 7 | 95 | 5 |
| 1–1.5 miles away | 88 | 12 | 80 | 20 |
| < 1 mile away | 82 | 18 | 89 | 11 |

Chi-square = 7.3690           Chi-square = 16.8079
d.f. = 2                      d.f. = 2
P = 0.0251                    P = 0.0002

of the disproportionate number of hazardous waste facilities in the city of Detroit (the city contains 50 percent of the 16 commercial hazardous waste facilities in the 3-county area but only about 20 percent of its population), or whether the same patterns exist both inside and outside the city. Thus, we repeated the above analysis: 1) once for the city of Detroit alone and 2) again for the suburban area (i.e., the 3-county area outside Detroit). The percentages in Table 2 indicate that the biases persist whether the city or the suburban area is examined by itself, although in the case of the City of Detroit the differences do not attain statistical significance. Although the suburban area contains very few minorities (the percentages of minority residents for Macomb, Oakland, and suburban Wayne Counties are 7 percent, 9 percent, and 5 percent, respectively, and

8 percent as a whole), it is there where the racial biases in the distribution of facilities are most pronounced (Table 2). Although generally the hazardous waste facilities are also disproportionately located in areas with high concentrations of people living below the poverty line, patterns are less clear when suburban areas and the city of Detroit are examined separately. In both the city and the suburban areas, the proportion of people who live below the poverty line is higher among people residing within a mile of a commercial hazardous waste facility than it is among those residing more than 1.5 miles away. However, in Detroit, the smallest concentrations of people living below the poverty line are in the neighborhoods that are between 1 and 1.5 miles from a facility; in the suburbs, neighborhoods that are between 1 and 1.5 miles from a facility have the highest concentrations (Table 2).

A major objective of our study was to examine the relative strength of the relationship of race and income on the distribution of commercial hazardous waste facilities in the Detroit area. In order to accomplish this objective, we used multiple linear regression analysis. We tested to see whether race (coded as 1=white and 0=minority) and income (measured in dollars) each had an independent relationship with the distance of residents to a commercial hazardous waste facility. And if so, which had the stronger relationship. We conducted the analysis in two ways. In the first analysis, the dependent variable used to measure distance to a site was an ordinal number which indicated the general proximity of the respondent to the site. Here, 1=within 1 mile, 2=between 1 mile and 1.5 miles, and 3=more than 1.5 miles away. In this analysis, all 793 respondents were included (and appropriately weighted to correct for the varying probability of selection into the study). In the second analysis, the precise distance of the respondent to the center of a facility (measured to the nearest 0.1 mile) was used as the dependent variable. In this latter analysis, only data from the 289 respondents in the oversample were used since precise distances to the commercial hazardous waste facilities were measured only for this group. Either approach yields similar results. The relationship between race and the location of commercial hazardous waste facilities in the Detroit area is independent of income in each of the analyses. And, important to the thesis of this paper, it is race which is the best predictor. In fact, in the second analysis, the relationship between the location of sites and income is no longer statistically significant.

## Conclusions

Review of 15 existing studies plus results of our Detroit area study provide clear and unequivocal evidence that income and racial biases in the distribution of environmental hazards exist. Our findings also appear to support the claims of those who have argued that race is more importantly related to the distribution of these hazards than income. Ultimately, knowing which is more important may be less relevant, however, than understanding the conditions associated with race and class that appear to consistently, if not inevitably, lead to inequitable exposure to environmental hazards and in understanding how these conditions can be addressed and how inequities in the distribution of environmental quality can be remedied.

Currently, there are no public policies in place which require monitoring equity in the distribution of environmental quality. Hence, policy makers have little knowledge about what the equity consequences are of the programs designed to control pollution in this country. Are some groups receiving fewer environmental and health remedies than others from existing programs? Have the risks to some actually increased as a result? If the social, economic, and political disadvantages faced by the poor and minorities that lead to environmental inequities are unlikely to be compensated any time soon, then it is clear that proactive government policies will be needed to address this issue. In the future, inequities in the distribution of environmental hazards will need to be monitored; existing policies and programs adjusted; and new programs designed in which enhancing environmental equity is a criterion for adoption.

A quarter of a century ago, the Kerner Commission (United States Government, 1968) warned that: "To continue present policies is to make permanent the division of our country into two societies: one largely Negro and poor, located in the central cities, the other predominantly white and affluent, located in the suburbs and in outlying areas." At the time that that warning was made, the EPA had not yet been created nor the nation's major environmental legislation yet passed. The terms "environmental racism" and "environmental justice" were unheard of. Results of our study and those of others indicate current environmental policies have allowed for separate societies differing in the quality of their respective environments. To know that these inequities exist but to do nothing about them is to perpetuate separate societies and will continue to leave the poor, blacks, and other minorities vulnerable to current and future environmental policy decisions.

## Notes

1.  One has to ask why minorities are disproportionately poor in the first place, however. Obviously, the answer is related to job and educational discrimination which contributes to the low pay and hence poor living conditions of minorities. Thus, the factor of race ultimately cannot be avoided.

2.  That housing discrimination is no insignificant influence on mobility was demonstrated in an ambitious national study by Denton and Massey (1988). Using U.S. Census Bureau data, they found that the degree of segregation found in black communities was not appreciably reduced by controlling for the income, education, and occupational status levels of the communities. This finding led Denton and Massey to conclude that race rather than income was the limiting factor on the mobility of blacks. "Clearly, black segregation in U.S. metropolitan areas cannot easily be attributed to socioeconomic differences from whites" (p. 805).

3.  The survey population for this special supplemental study includes all households who live within a 1.5 mile radial zone of the 16 designated commercial hazardous waste facilities (14 existing and 2 proposed). From this survey population a two-stage equal probability sample of households was selected. The distribution of sampled households in the 16 zones which comprise the survey population is proportional to the total number of households which reside in each zone. Zones surrounding commercial hazardous waste facilities which have low population densities are expected to have smaller numbers of sampled households than zones with higher household densities. Although all households in the survey population had an equal chance of selection for the study, densities in several of the 16 commercial hazardous waste facility zones are suf-

ficiently low that no sample observations were in fact selected. However, as inference from the sample is to the entire population of people living in all 16 zones, the sample selected is representative of the entire population of residents living within 1.5 miles of these 16 commercial hazardous waste facility zones.

4. The U.S. Census Bureau definition was used here.

## References

Asch, P., and J. J. Seneca. 1978. "Some Evidence on the Distribution of Air Quality." *Land Economics* 54(3): 278-97.

Berry, B. J., L. S. Caris, D. Gaskill, C. P. Kaplan, J. Piccinini, N. Planert, J. H. Rendall III, and A. de Ste. Phalle. 1977. *The Social Burdens of Environmental Pollution: A Comparative Metropolitan Data Source.* Cambridge, MA: Ballinger Publishing Co.

Bullard, R. D. 1983. "Solid Waste Sites and the Houston Black Community." *Sociological Inquiry* 53(Spring): 273-88.

_____. 1990. *Dumping in Dixie: Race, Class, and Environmental Quality.* Boulder, CO: Westview Press.

Bullard, R. D., and B. H. Wright. 1987. "Environmentalism and the Politics of Equity: Emergent Trends in the Black Community." *Mid-American Review of Sociology* 12: 21-38.

Burch, W. R. 1976. "The Peregrine Falcon and the Urban Poor: Some Sociological Interrelations." In P. Richerson and J. McEvoy, eds. *Human Ecology, An Environmental Approach.* Belmont, CA: Duxbury Press.

Council on Environmental Quality. 1971. *The Second Annual Report of the Council on Environmental Quality.* Washington, DC: U. S. Government Printing Office.

Davies, J. C., and B. S. Davies. 1975. *The Politics of Pollution, 2nd Edition.* Indianapolis, IN: Pegasus.

Denton, N. A., and D. S. Massey. 1988. "Residential Segregation of Blacks, Hispanics, and Asians by Socioeconomic Status and Generation." *Social Science Quarterly* 69(4): 797-817.

Feagin, J. R., and C. B. Feagin. 1978. *Discrimination American Style: Institutional Racism and Sexism, 2nd Edition.* Malabar, FL: Krieger Publishing Company.

Fessler, P. 1990. "A Quarter-Century of Activism Erected a Bulwark of Laws." *Congressional Quarterly Weekly Report* 48(3): 153-56.

Freeman, A. M. 1972. "The Distribution of Environmental Quality." In A. V. Kneese and B. T. Bower, eds. *Environmental Quality Analysis.* Baltimore, MD: Johns Hopkins University Press for Resources for the Future.

Gelobter, M. 1987. *The Distribution of Outdoor Air Pollution by Income and Race: 1970-1984.* Master's Thesis, Energy and Resource Group. Berkeley, CA: University of California.

_____. 1992. "Toward a Model of Environmental Discrimination." In B. Bryant and P. Mohai, eds. *Race and The Incidence of Environmental Hazards: A Time for Discourse.* Boulder, CO: Westview Press.

Gianessi, L., H. M. Peskin, and E. Wolff. 1979. "The Distributional Effects of Uniform Air Pollution Policy in the U.S." *Quarterly Journal of Economics* (May): 281-301.

Handy, F. 1977. "Income and Air Quality in Hamilton, Ontario." *Alternatives* 6(3): 18-24.

Harrison, D., Jr. 1975. *Who Pays for Clean Air: The Cost and Benefit Distribution of Automobile Emission Standards.* Cambridge, MA: Ballinger.

Kish, L. 1949. "A Procedure for Objective Respondent Selection within the Household." *American Statistical Association Journal* (September): 380-87.

Kruvant, W. J. 1975. "People, Energy, and Pollution." In D. K. Newman and D. Day, eds. *The American Energy Consumer.* Cambridge, MA: Ballinger.

Lee, C. 1992. "Toxic Waste and Race in the United States." In B. Bryant and P. Mohai, eds. *Race and The Incidence of Environmental Hazards: A Time for Discourse.* Boulder, CO: Westview Press.

Mohai, P. 1985. "Public Concern and Elite Involvement in Environmental-Conservation Issues." *Social Science Quarterly* 66(4): 820-38.

_____. 1990. "Black Environmentalism." *Social Science Quarterly* 71(4): 744-65.

Mohai, P., and B. Bryant. 1989. "Race and the Incidence of Environmental Hazards: A Proposal for the 1990 Detroit Area Study." School of Natural Resources. Ann Arbor, MI: University of Michigan.

United Church of Christ. 1987. *Toxic Wastes and Race in the United States: A National Report on the Racial and Socio-Economic Characteristics of Communities with Hazardous Waste Sites.* New York: Commission for Racial Justice, United Church of Christ.

U. S. General Accounting Office. 1983. *Siting of Hazardous Waste Landfills and Their Correlation with Racial and Economic Status of Surrounding Communities.* Washington, DC: U. S. General Accounting Office.

U. S. Government Printing Office. 1968. *Report of the National Advisory Commission on Civil Disorders.* Washington, DC: U.S. Government Printing Office.

Weisskopf, M. 1992. "Minorities' Pollution Risk Is Debated." *The Washington Post,* January 16.

West, P.C., J.M. Fly, F. Larkin, and R. Marans. 1992. "Minority Anglers and Toxic Fish Consumption: Evidence from a State-Wide Survey of Michigan." In B. Bryant and P. Mohai, eds. *Race and The Incidence of Environmental Hazards: A Time for Discourse.* Boulder, CO: Westview Press.

Zupan, J. M. 1973. *The Distribution of Air Quality in the New York Region.* Baltimore, MD: Johns Hopkins University Press for Resources for the Future, Inc.

# 2

# Studies Used to Prove Charges of Environmental Racism Are Flawed

Douglas L. Anderton, Andy B. Anderson,
Peter H. Rossi, John Michael Oakes, Michael R. Fraser,
Eleanor W. Weber, and Edward J. Calabrese

*Douglas L. Anderton is a professor of sociology and director of the So-cial and Demographic Research Institute (SADRI) at the University of Massachusetts at Amherst (UMass). Anderton has published a variety of books and articles on research methodologies and demographic trends and is currently researching questions of environmental equity. Andy B. Anderson is professor of sociology at UMass and a member of SADRI. Peter H. Rossi is S.A. Rice Professor Emeritus of Sociology at UMass and director emeritus of SADRI. John Michael Oakes and Michael R. Fraser are doctoral students in sociology at UMass and researchers at SADRI. Eleanor W. Weber is database administrator for SADRI. Edward J. Calabrese is professor of public health and director of the Northeast Environmental Health Center at UMass.*

Studies assert that industrial waste treatment, storage, and disposal facilities (TSDFs) are disproportionately located in minority neighborhoods, unjustly exposing the residents of such communities to environmental hazards. Because they are regional in scope and define communities too broadly in size, these studies are not definitive. The present study, which was funded by Chemical Waste Management, attempts to rectify these flaws by using national census data and more realistic definitions of neighborhoods. Analysis of the data reveals that, in general, race is less positively correlated with the presence of TSDFs than are economic variables such as unemployment and employment in industrial occupations. In sum, the evidence does not support the charge of environmental inequity.

In the past two decades, American society has become increasingly conscious that the waste products of its advanced technology can pose dangers to the health of citizens and to the viability of the ecosystem on

Douglas L. Anderton, Andy B. Anderson, Peter H. Rossi, John Michael Oakes, Michael R. Fraser, Eleanor W. Weber, and Edward J. Calabrese, "Hazardous Waste Facilities: 'Environmental Equity' Issues in Metropolitan Areas," *Evaluation Review* (vol. 18, no. 2), pp. 123-40, ©1994 Sage Publications. Reprinted by permission of Sage Publications, Inc..

which all depend. This concern has given rise to a number of salient policy issues centering around how best to minimize those dangers in efficient and equitable ways. This article presents new and divergent findings related to some of the equity issues in the location of hazardous waste facilities. In particular, we investigate the extent to which the geographic distribution of hazardous waste facilities may disproportionately expose neighborhoods with greater numbers of racial and ethnic minority residents to potential risks arising from such industrial activities.

*It is doubtful that many Americans would want a TSDF [treatment, storage, and disposal facility] as a near neighbor and many would prefer not to be within miles of a site.*

Safety standards for the commercial disposal and/or long-term storage of many hazardous wastes are mandated by law. The Environmental Protection Agency (EPA) is the regulatory agency primarily charged with oversight of hazardous waste facilities. Commercial waste disposal firms typically operate several different Treatment, Storage, and Disposal Facilities (TSDFs) constituting locations at which hazardous wastes are either destroyed, stored, or held for transshipment. Some firms maintain their own facilities rather than relying on the service industry.

It is doubtful that many Americans would want a TSDF as a near neighbor and many would prefer not to be within miles of a site. Concern over the location of waste-handling facilities has provoked a political issue involving whether TSDFs, and any plausible associated risks, may be disproportionately located in neighborhoods with minority racial and ethnic groups. Inequitable exposure of minorities to environmental hazards has been labeled "environmental racism." These concerns are subsumed under the more general questions of environmental equity, which have evoked major policy attention as well as a discussion of constitutional and other legal issues in major law reviews (Chase 1993; Lazarus 1993).

The issue of equity in siting is a complicated one. To begin with, how much potential risk is generated by a TSDF has not been established nor has the relationship been determined between such risks and distance from a site. A number of epidemiological studies of areas around toxic waste sites have been carried out (e.g., Andelman and Underhill 1987; Deane et al. 1989; Grisham 1986). Most available epidemiological studies offer little conclusive evidence, although several case studies show there is some evidence of harm in proximity to toxic waste sites, enough to merit further study (e.g., Geschwind 1992; Geschwind et al. 1992).[1] As usual, the results of case studies have to be interpreted with caution. Confounding factors and differences across sites make a more general evaluation of health effects and risk assessment difficult, if not impossible. Further problems in such assessments arise because TSDFs vary in the kinds of hazardous wastes processed and in the amount of processing taking place. It is likely that the distribution of risks around a site varies accordingly.

Although most of the attention in the controversy over TSDF siting has centered around their potential negative effects, there are also potential positive ones, including employment opportunities for local residents and lowered rents and real estate prices. The net effects of TSDF siting on a neighborhood may be properly conceived of as a balance that considers negative effects as offset to some degree by positive ones.

Although in the long run we will need to know the extent to which specific TSDFs are associated with higher levels of morbidity and mortality and what are safe distances from such sites, for the present discussion our current lack of knowledge is not relevant. The current political debate over siting assumes that TSDFs generate significant effects and that those effects decrease with distance from the site.

There are also issues concerning what constitutes equity and inequity in site location. One view is that site location equity can be defined as the outcome of siting processes in which the population compositions of sites and surrounding areas played no roles. For example, TSDF sites may be chosen because of proximity to customers, real estate prices, and zoning regulations. As long as all qualifying sites have equal chances of being selected, equity is assured. That is, neighborhoods populated by high proportions of minorities would be no more likely to be selected than other areas that are equally suitable as sites. It is important to note that sites with high proportions of minorities may incidentally be more likely to be selected because they are more desirable as locations. In this view, equity is in the blindness of site selection processes to population composition of potential sites.

An alternative view of equity assumes that in siting TSDFs, a strategy should be adopted that ensures that sites with high percentages of minorities should not appear with any greater frequency than any other kind of site. Accordingly, if TSDF sites are found to be more frequently located in or near minority neighborhoods, then a condition of environmental inequity exists.

It should be noted that a finding that TSDF sites are in fact more likely to be located in or near minority areas can be interpreted as equitable or not depending on which definition of equity one adopts. However, if findings are otherwise, all definitions converge on the interpretation that the evidence does not support inequity.

This article does not take a stand on how equity should be defined. However, it does take the position that if our findings indicate that sites are not in or near areas with relatively high proportions of minority residents, then there is no evidence of inequity in siting.

## Prior studies

Three previous empirical studies of the population characteristics of the areas surrounding hazardous waste sites have received considerable public attention. The first was conducted by the General Accounting Office (GAO 1983) "to determine the correlation between the location of hazardous waste landfills and the racial and economic status of surrounding communities" (p. 2). GAO researchers compiled zip-code-level population data for areas surrounding four hazardous waste facilities in EPA Region 4, composed of South Atlantic states. The GAO found that the majority of the population in census areas containing three of the four facilities was black.

The second and most widely discussed empirical study was sponsored by the United Church of Christ's (UCC) Commission for Racial Justice in 1986 to determine the racial and socioeconomic characteristics of Americans living in residential areas surrounding commercial hazardous waste facilities (Commission for Racial Justice 1987). Like the GAO study, the UCC study used five-digit zip code areas as communities. Three population measures were central to the study: percentage of minority population[2] (blacks plus Hispanics), mean household income, and mean value of owner-occupied housing. The last two variables were employed as indicators of socioeconomic status (p. 10).

The main UCC (1987) analysis compared the 1980 population characteristics of zip code areas containing TSDFs to all other zip codes in the continental United States.[3] The UCC report found that zip code areas with at least one commercial TSDF operating in 1986 had an average proportion of minority residents twice that in areas without TSDF facilities. In addition, the socioeconomic differences between them "were not as significant as the mean minority percentage of the population" (p. 13). These results led UCC to conclude, "Race proved to be the most significant among variables tested in association with the location of commercial hazardous waste facilities. This represents a consistent national pattern" (p. xiii).

*Clearly, changing the area definitions can result in radical changes in findings concerning environmental equity.*

A third empirical study, conducted by Mohai and Bryant (1992), used a sample survey to assess racial biases in location of commercial hazardous waste facilities within three counties, including and surrounding the city of Detroit. The researchers employed the Detroit area study, sponsored by the University of Michigan, to draw a household probability sample of the three counties, with an oversampling of respondents within 1.5 miles of each of 16 commercial waste disposal sites in the three counties. The study found that 48% of all the persons living within a mile of a TSDF were black, compared to 39% who lived in the 1-mile to 1.5-mile zone and 18% of those living more than 1.5 miles from a TSDF. They also found that race differences associated with distance from a TSDF were greater than socioeconomic status differences.

The three empirical studies summarized above have received considerable attention and have been influential in shaping national environmental policy. Two national conferences (Commission for Racial Justice 1991; Mohai and Bryant 1992) were convened to review research and formulate strategies for obtaining environmental justice.

The EPA now requires data on risk to minorities to be submitted in environmental impact statements. In July 1990, the EPA formed an Environmental Equity Workgroup to assess the evidence that racial minority and low-income communities bear a higher risk burden than the general population and to consider what the EPA might do about it (EPA 1992, 2). In their 1992 report to the EPA administrator, the workgroup cited the GAO report ( 1983), the UCC (1987) report, and the Michigan Conference on "Race and Incidence of Environmental Hazards" (Mohai and Bryant 1992). Early in 1993, the EPA set up an Office of Environmental Equity. In a recent (Grossfield 1993) lead story in the *Boston Globe*, Vice President Albert Gore was quoted as saying, "Race is the single most accurate predictor of the location of hazardous waste sites."

Although it is heartening to learn that the policy arena pays some attention to empirical social research, these three studies are far from definitive. The GAO study is a collection of cases that cannot be generalized to the entire United States. The UCC study is national in scope but rests on an operational definition of community (zip codes) that may be too large. The Detroit study is also a limited case study carried out in a single metropolitan region dominated by a central city that is 76% black. We do not assert that these studies are wrong, but they are not definitive.

## Research design and data sources

The analytic problem to be addressed is whether TSDF sites are more likely to be located in or near to neighborhood communities with larger proportions of blacks or Hispanics. To address this problem, it is necessary to define community in operational terms. Because equity issues are ultimately concerned with potential risk or harm from TSDFs, the area chosen for analysis should correspond to the likely areal distribution of possible harm from a TSDF,[4] but there is little solid evidence of specific harmful effects of living near TSDFs. Furthermore, TSDFs have a wide variety of potential effects (e.g., health hazards, air pollution, land opportunity costs, employment opportunities), each with unknown and, no doubt, different gradients of influence. Consequently, there are no firm guidelines on how to define areas that are subject to the potential effects of a TSDF.

In the absence of clear indications about which areal unit to adopt as a unit of analysis, the sensible strategy is to choose the smallest available areal units that can then be aggregated into larger units if necessary. Beginning with too large a geographic unit of analysis invites the possibility of aggregation errors and ecological fallacies (i.e., reaching conclusions from a larger unit of analysis that do not hold true in analyses of smaller, more refined, geographic units).

There are also constraints on the adoption of an operational definition of neighborhood that arise from the limitations of existing data sets. The only data sets that contain population composition information on all areas of the United States originate in the decennial census[5] (U.S. Bureau of the Census 1980). The smallest areal units for which detailed social and economic data are readily available in the census data sets are tracts, units that can be aggregated to larger units, such as cities, or counties.[6] Overall, census tracts have an average population of about 4,000 persons and a median land area (in 1990) of about 0.74 square miles.[7] Tract boundaries are set up by local census tract committees with instructions to "reflect the structure of the metropolis as viewed by those most familiar with it" (Bogue 1985, 137) and hence are more likely to be drawn to reflect local ideas of homogeneous neighborhoods. Because census tracts come closest to conforming to the definition of neighborhood communities, cover the places most likely to be candidates for TSDF locations, and can be aggregated, we used census tracts as basic areal units.

Prior to the 1990 census, tracts were only defined for Standard Metropolitan Statistical Areas (SMSAs), consisting of cities with populations of 50,000 or more and their surrounding counties or urbanized areas, omitting many rural areas, smaller cities, and small towns. About 15% of TSDFs arc located outside SMSAs and hence cannot be studied through a research strategy employing census tracts as units of analysis.

Our analysis is further confined to those SMSAs in which at least one

TSDF is located. We compare characteristics of census tracts (and various aggregations of such tracts) in SMSAs in which TSDFs were located to other tracts in the same SMSAs in which facilities were not located.TSDFs located in portions of the country not tracted in the 1980 census (approximately 15% of all TSDFs) are not studied here, although future analyses will include them. A total of 47,311 tracts are identified in the 1980 census, containing approximately 80% of the U.S.population in 300 SMSAs (U.S. Bureau of the Census 1980). Of these, 32,003 tracts were in SMSAs of the 48 contiguous states with at least one commercial TSDF.

---

*TSDFs are no more likely to be located in tracts with higher percentages of blacks and Hispanics than in other tracts.*

---

To carry out the analysis, it was also necessary to identify those specific tracts containing commercial TSDFs. This study includes only TSDFs that opened for business prior to 1990 and that were still operating in 1992. The tract locations of TSDFs were obtained using information maintained by the EPA and the Environmental Institute (1992), as supplemented by a telephone survey of TSDFs and computerized geocoding.[8]

We selected eight census tract characteristics for the purposes of this article.[9] Two variables are used to characterize racial and ethnic composition: percentage black persons and percentage Hispanic persons.[10] Three variables summarize the economic conditions of the population within geographic areas: percentage of non-farm families of four at or below 1979 poverty line, the percentage of households receiving public assistance income in 1979, and the percentage of all males (aged 16+) employed in the civilian labor force. Finally, three variables reflect industrial and housing characteristics of areas: the percentage employed in precision production, craft, and repair occupations and operator, fabricator and laborer occupations; the mean value of owner-occupied housing stock; and the percentage owner-occupied housing units built prior to 1960.

## Analysis

We compare selected social and economic characteristics of tracts containing TSDFs to those of other tracts in Table 1. The results are considerably different from prior studies: There are slightly fewer blacks in TSDF tracts (14.5% vs. 15.2%), but the difference is not statistically significant.[11] There is a slightly larger percentage of Hispanics in TSDF tracts (9% vs. 8%), but again the difference is not clearly significant. Two indicators of economic status—percentage below the poverty level and percentage with public assistance income—do not differ, but significantly fewer males of employable age are employed in the TSDF tracts. There are also more people employed in industrial occupations in TSDF tracts (38% vs. 31%), and housing values are lower in TSDF tracts even though fewer of the houses were built before 1960.

In short, the percentages of black, Hispanic, and economically disadvantaged in tract populations do not seem to distinguish between the tracts, but there are strong indications that the TSDF tracts are composed of residents who are working class in socioeconomic status, who are em-

### Table 1. Comparison of TSDF Tracts
### to Tracts Without TSDFs in all SMSAs

| Variable | Tract Means | | Cases | | t Test | Significance Probability |
|---|---|---|---|---|---|---|
| | TSDF | Other | TSDF | Other | | |
| Percentage black | 14.54 | 15.20 | 408 | 31,595 | –0.53 | 0.60 |
| Percentage Hispanic | 9.41 | 7.74 | 408 | 31,595 | 1.88 | 0.06 |
| Percentage families below poverty | 14.50 | 13.94 | 404 | 31,269 | 0.96 | 0.34 |
| Percentage households on public assistance | 9.51 | 9.01 | 406 | 31,306 | 1.12 | 0.26 |
| Percentage males employed | 91.75 | 92.73 | 406 | 31,401 | –3.06 | 0.00 |
| Percentage industrial employment | 38.60 | 30.61 | 406 | 31,413 | 13.36 | 0.00 |
| Average value of owned housing ($) | 47,120.15 | 58,352.21 | 393 | 30,028 | –8.84 | 0.00 |
| Percentage housing built before 1960 | 55.73 | 59.80 | 406 | 31,317 | –2.96 | 0.00 |

NOTE: TSDF = treatment, storage, and disposal of hazardous wastes facilities. SMSA = Standard Metropolitan Statistical Area. Average area characteristics are compared using *t* tests for means with unequal variances. The number of cases varies because some tracts had no residents with the relevant characteristics (e.g., the percentage of families below poverty level can be computed only for tracts with residential families). TSDF tracts are single tracts containing one or more TSDF sites.

ployed to a greater extent in industrial occupations, and who live in less expensive and more recently built housing.

To determine whether environmental inequities differ for large cities, the analysis is repeated for the 25 largest SMSAs, with the results shown in Table 2. For these cities, TSDF tracts have, in fact, a significantly lower percentage of blacks. However, TSDF tracts in these large cities have a significantly higher percentage of Hispanic residents. Again, TSDF tracts have significantly more unemployment and higher levels of industrial employment, with cheaper and more recently built houses.

Census tracts are smaller than zip code areas analyzed in earlier studies. To test sensitivity of these findings to the size of the area analyzed, a larger area was constructed for comparative analysis, consisting of all tracts with at least 50% of their areas falling within a 2.5-mile radius of the center of a tract in which a TSDF was located. The percentage black in these larger areas is significantly higher than in other tracts (25% vs. 14%). Hispanics constitute a higher percentage, 11% versus 7% for other tracts. Socioeconomic characteristics of the larger TSDF areas are also different. There are more families below the poverty line (19% vs. 13%), more households with public assistance income (13% vs. 8%), and lower levels of male employment (90% vs. 93%), all differences which are statistically significant in the direction prior studies suggest. In these larger TSDF areas, industrial employment remains significantly higher (36% vs. 30%), and housing is older with significantly lower average value.

These relationships are even more dramatic for the 25 largest SMSAs. Except for the value of housing, the differences between the larger TSDF areas and the rest of the tracts are at least as great as those reported for all SMSAs.

Clearly, changing the area definitions can result in radical changes in

### Table 2.  Comparison of TSDF Tracts to Tracts Without TSDFs in 25 Largest SMSAs

| Variable | Tract Means | | Cases | | t Test | Significance Probability |
|---|---|---|---|---|---|---|
| | TSDF | Other | TSDF | Other | | |
| Percentage black | 12.23 | 16.43 | 150 | 17,406 | –2.18 | 0.03 |
| Percentage Hispanic | 13.88 | 10.05 | 150 | 17,406 | 2.25 | 0.03 |
| Percentage families below poverty | 12.46 | 13.53 | 149 | 17,211 | –1.21 | 0.23 |
| Percentage households on public assistance | 9.23 | 9.64 | 150 | 17,230 | –0.49 | 0.63 |
| Percentage males employed | 91.43 | 92.71 | 150 | 17,288 | –2.26 | 0.02 |
| Percentage industrial employment | 37.08 | 28.95 | 150 | 17,300 | 7.58 | 0.00 |
| Average value of owned housing ($) | 55,980.13 | 65,764.10 | 145 | 16,323 | –3.89 | 0.00 |
| Percentage housing built before 1960 | 55.96 | 62.64 | 150 | 17,236 | –2.68 | 0.01 |

NOTE: TSDF – treatment, storage, and disposal of hazardous wastes facilities. SMSA = Standard Metropolitan Statistical Area. Average area characteristics are compared using t tests for means with unequal variances. The number of cases varies because some tracts had no residents with the relevant characteristics (e.g., the percentage of families below poverty level can be computed only for tracts with residential families). TSDF tracts are single tracts containing one or more TSDF sites.

findings concerning environmental equity and may account for the discrepancy between the findings of Table 1 and prior research. Going from single tracts to aggregates of tracts caught in the 2.5-mile radius around a TSDF is, however, a considerable jump in size. To elaborate further, we use only the 25 largest SMSAs and, in Table 3, break down the aggregation into the following exclusive and successive areas around TSDFs: (1) tracts containing TSDFs; (2) tracts abutting TSDF tracts; (3) nonabutting tracts within the 2.5-mile radius around the TSDF tracts; and (4) all other tracts beyond the 2.5-mile radius within the SMSAs.[12]

The findings of Table 3 indicate that TSDF and abutting tracts are very much alike in composition and socioeconomic status.[13] It is the farther distant, nonabutting tracts within the 2.5-mile radius that contain significantly larger proportions of blacks, 32.7% in stark contrast to the 14.7% in the remainder of the SMSA tracts. In contrast, the percentage of Hispanics is about the same everywhere within the 2.5-mile radius, between 14% and 15% Hispanic in contrast to 9.3% in the remainder of the SMSA tracts.

Most other variables progressively increase or decrease when moving from the TSDF to more distant tracts. All of the socioeconomic variables show that the nonabutting tracts are the poorest in the 2.5-mile radius circle. Industrial employment is greatest in the TSDF tracts where housing values are lowest and the newest housing is found.

Further confounding any claim of national-level results, the patterns described above vary considerably within regions of the country. TSDF tracts have significantly lower percentages of persons black in the North Mid-Atlantic, East North Central, and West South Central regions (i.e., EPA Regions, 2, 5, and 67) and significantly higher percentages of blacks

**Table 3. Breakdown of Areas Surrounding
TSDF Sites in 25 Largest SMSAs**

| | Within Radius of 2.5 Miles | | | |
|---|---|---|---|---|
| Variable | TSDF Tracts | Abutting Tracts | Nonabutting Tracts | All Other Tracts |
| Percentage black | 12.23 | 15.76 | 32.70* | 14.67 |
| Percentage Hispanic | 13.88* | 14.53* | 14.94* | 9.32 |
| Percentage families below poverty | 12.46 | 14.53* | 20.39* | 12.72 |
| Percentage households on public assistance | 9.23 | 11.13* | 16.49* | 8.81 |
| Percentage males employed | 91.43* | 90.93* | 88.40* | 93.26 |
| Percentage industrial employment | 37.08* | 36.82* | 35.17* | 27.91 |
| Average value of owned housing ($) | 55,980* | 53,414* | 50,227* | 60,012 |
| Percentage housing built before 1960 | 55.96* | 64.48* | 78.62* | 60.80 |
| Approximate $N$[a] | 150 | 667 | 1,662 | 15,077 |

NOTE: TSDF = treatment, storage, and disposal of hazardous wastes facilities. SMSA = Standard Metropolitan Statistical Area.
a. For some variables the $N$ is smaller because of missing values for a small percentage of tracts.
*Contrast with all other tracts (last column) is significant at .05 level.

in TSDF tracts only in the South Atlantic region (i.e., EPA Regions 2, 3, 4) with higher percentages Hispanic only in the TSDF tracts of the Southwest (i.e., EPA Region 9). Thus higher percentages of blacks and Hispanics are each found only in TSDF tracts of a single region (i.e., the South Atlantic and Southwest, respectively) where they are most highly represented in the general population.

Finally, to confirm these findings and estimate the relative importance of the competing associations requires multivariate analyses. The coefficients shown in Table 4 are changes in the log of the odds of the area's containing a TSDF for each unit change in the independent variable. A positive (negative) coefficient for a variable means the chance that the area contains a TSDF becomes greater (less) with increases in that variable, net of the influences of all the other variables included.[14]

The logistic regression results shown in the first column of Table 4 use being a TSDF tract as the dependent measure. Neither the percentage black or Hispanic in the tract is significantly associated with tracts containing one or more TSDFs. Most of the socioeconomic variables have coefficients that are insignificant, but the percentage of males employed is negatively related to being a TSDF tract. The percentage employed in industrial occupations has the greatest positive effect on whether an area will contain a TSDF and the percentage of homes built before 1960 has a negative effect. These findings are largely consistent with those of Table 1.

The second column of Table 4 contains results of a logistic regression for whether a census tract is within a larger TSDF area. The percentage black and percentage Hispanic within a tract are both significantly positively related to being a larger TSDF area. However, even in these larger areas, the two largest coefficients are the negative effect of percentage employed and the positive effect of percentage employed in industrial firms. All effects in the regression are again similar to those in Table 2.

Overall, the multivariate analysis supports our earlier findings. The

**Table 4.  Logistic Regressions of TSDF
Present in an Area on Selected Variables**

| Variable | Coefficient | |
| --- | --- | --- |
| | TSDF Tract | 2.5-Mile Radius |
| Percentage black | –0.0009 | 0.0045* |
| Percentage Hispanic | –0.0001 | 0.0071* |
| Percentage families below poverty | –0.0210* | –0.0058* |
| Percentage households on public assistance | 0.0078 | 0.0057 |
| Percentage males employed | –0.0253* | –0.0359* |
| Percentage industrial employment | 0.0468* | 0.0229* |
| Average value of owned housing ($) | –0.0000* | –0.0000 |
| Percentage housing built before 1960 | –0.0107* | 0.0135* |
| Constant | –2.4181* | –0.1677 |
| Chi-square | 186.01 | 1975.95 |
| Probability > Chi-square | 0.000 | 0.000 |
| N | 30,413 | 30,413 |

NOTE: TSDF = treatment, storage, and disposal of hazardous wastes facilities.
*Indicates statistical significance, $p \leq 0.05$.

most significant effects in each case are not those of percentage black or percentage Hispanic, but of unemployment and industrial employment within the area. For census tracts, the effects of percentage black and of percentage Hispanic are not significant. However, in much larger areas, both variables appear to be associated with the presence of TSDFs.

## Conclusion

Three major implications are to be drawn from our study. First, the appearance of equity in the location of TSDFs depends heavily on how areas of potential impact or interest are defined. Second, using census tract areas, TSDFs are no more likely to be located in tracts with higher percentages of blacks and Hispanics than in other tracts. Third, the most significant and consistent effect on TSDF location of those we considered is that TSDFs are located in areas with larger proportions of workers employed in industrial activities, a finding that is consistent with a plausibly rational motivation to locate near other industrial facilities or markets. Whether or not this interpretation is correct cannot be fully sustained in this viewpoint but requires more direct evidence. Research currently under way is directed at examining the industrial composition of TSDF site areas.

Although findings vary with different geographic units of analysis, a generally consistent theme emerges. If the scope of the analysis is restricted to the 25 largest SMSAs, tracts with higher percentages of blacks are less likely, whereas those with high percentages of Hispanics are slightly more likely, to be TSDF locations. If much larger areas are analyzed, the findings change dramatically, with TSDF areas having higher percentages of blacks and Hispanics than other tracts. When these larger areas are broken down further, tracts adjacent to TSDF tracts are found to be like the TSDF tracts themselves. It is only in tracts on the periphery of the 2.5-mile radius circle around TSDFs that the proportions of black residents are significantly larger. Findings concerning persons of Hispanic origins differ, with larger proportions of Hispanics found near TSDFs in a variety of geographic comparisons. However, only in the single regions of the country in which the black and Hispanic populations are most well represented is there evidence that TSDFs are more likely to be located in tracts with greater proportions of these minorities. Certainly these minorities are not the most immediately exposed to the potential hazards of TSDFs throughout most of the country. None of these effects appears to be as consistent or significant as the finding that TSDFs are most likely to be attracted to industrial tract areas.

---

*Within metropolitan areas containing TSDFs, we find no nationally consistent and convincing evidence of . . . environmental inequity.*

---

The analyses presented here also rest on assumptions concerning those parts of the United States that are relevant as comparisons to areas potentially affected by TSDF locations. By restricting our inquiry to SMSAs that had at least one TSDF, all of the analyses presented here compare areas with and without TSDFs only in those large metropolitan areas (SMSAs) of the United States with at least one such facility. In these comparisons, it is not our intent to define equity among social groups as merely an equal exposure to the likelihood of living near a TSDF. Instead, we have followed other researchers in seeking to assess whether the location of facilities suggests inequity in such risks. Within metropolitan areas containing TSDFs, we find no nationally consistent and convincing evidence of such environmental inequity.

We believe our findings show that TSDFs are more likely to be attracted to industrial tracts and those tracts do not generally have a greater number of minority residents. Why areas located at the fringe of a 2.5-mile radius from TSDFs should be more likely to have relatively high percentages of minority residents, we are unable to account for from the analyses presented. It appears likely that these findings reflect broader residential patterns largely unaffected by, and ineffective on, decisions of where to locate TSDFs. We are continuing to investigate this interesting question. Until that question is resolved, we must conclude that the evidence for environmental inequity is, at best, mixed in its message.

## Notes

1. Several other, less detailed, studies suggest similar conclusions. In a study of 606 households located near the Stringfellow Waste Disposal Site in Riverside County, California, researchers found an elevation in disease when this group was compared to selected comparison groups (Baker et al. 1988). Types of diseases reported include "ear infections, bronchitis, asthma, angina pectoris, skin rashes, blurred vision, nausea, frequent urination" (p. 325) and other intestinal disorders. Stephens (181, 55) reports that residents of Fullerton, California, who lived near the abandoned McColl disposal site reported similar problems, including difficulties in breathing, headaches, and dizziness, and they complained of foul odors.

2. These are not mutually exclusive population categories. Hence summing them leads to some degree of double counting, especially in areas where there are significant numbers of black Hispanics, as on the East coast.

3. Some 400 zip codes were eliminated because they had no population or because they were codes for mail order firms, schools, and so on.

4. Of course, equity issues might be raised over possible benefits (e.g., employment) from TSDFs as well.

5. The census bureau routinely provides machine-readable data files at different levels of aggregation, including tracts, counties, and states. Zip code files are available for some census years compiled by private vendors from census sources.

6. A limited amount of social and economic data are available for blocks, an areal unit which is difficult to analyze and which we believe to be too small to be useful.

7. There are considerable variations both in tract population sizes and tract areas. Although the median tract population size in the 1980 SMSAs included in the analyses was 3,861 persons, the interquartile range was from 2,601 to 5,405 persons. In contrast, zip code areas for 1980 contained, on the average, nearly twice as many (close to 6,500) persons. Tract areas, available only in 1990, also varied widely. Excluding very large outliers (tracts larger than 80 square miles) the median was .733 and the mean 3.107 square miles.

8. Although the National Resource Conservation and Recovery Act (RCRA) requires the EPA to collect and publish data on hazardous waste production, transport, and disposal facilities, it does not provide information needed for our research. Consequently, we used the latest available Environmental Institutes' (1992) *Environmental Services Directory* (ESD) as our primary source on TSDF listings. The 1992 ESD contained 454 commercial TSDFs that met the criteria of having begun operation before 1990 and being located in SMSAs that had been tracted for the 1980s census. Using a telephone survey to clarify ambiguous or missing information, we were able to geocode census tract locations of 98% (all but 8) and obtain dates of establishment for 92.5% (all but 34) of the commercial TSDFs.

9. A variety of causal arguments or hypotheses might suggest a different subset of variables. Our selection was intended only to illustrate interesting differences, to address variables already raised in prior research, and not to suggest any causal primacy of variables selected.

10. The sum of the percentages who identified themselves as Mexican, Puerto Rican, Cuban, and other Spanish persons.

11. Throughout, a significance probability of at least .05 is used to determine statistical significance. Where the significance probability is within the range of .10 to .05, qualifying phrases such as *not highly* or *somewhat* are used to convey marginal possible significance.

It should be noted, of course, that a difference can be statistically significant without being substantively significant. The difference between TSDF tracts and other tracts with respect to percentage Hispanic, for example was significant with a *p* value of .06. The actual percentage difference was less than 2%. Statistical significance only means, roughly, that we think the difference is not due to random error but rather is a genuine difference. Whether that small percentage difference is practically or substantively significant is another question.

12. This classification had to be accomplished by visual inspection of tract maps for each of the SMSAs. Hence the restriction to the 25 largest SMSAs. It should be remembered that tracts, and hence the areas produced by aggregations, are irregular in shape.

13. TSDF and abutting tracts are significantly different only with respect to the proportions of housing built before 1960, the former containing less housing built before 1960.

14. We are ignoring problems of spatial autocorrelation, a condition which can produce an error structure that is not $\sigma^2 I$. The effect is similar to autocorrelation in time series data: the coefficients are not biased but the standard errors are biased downward, leading to $p$ values lower than they should be. However, the standard GLS solutions are not practical here because it would require an omega matrix of over 30,000 × 30,000. Moreover, spatial autocorrelation generally does not follow a simple structure, such as the first order autoregressive process often assumed with time series data (Anselin 1988).

## References

Andelman, Julian B., and Dwight W. Underhill, eds. 1987. *Health effects from hazardous waste sites.* Chelsea, MI: Lewis.

Anselin, Luc, 1988. *Spatial econometrics: Methods and models.* Dordrecht: Kluwer.

Baker, Dean B., Sander Greenland, James Mendlein, and Patricia Harmon. 1988. A health study of two communities near the Stringfellow Waste Disposal Site. *Archives of Environmental Health* 43(5): 325-34.

Bogue, Donald J. 1985. *The population of the United States: Historical trends and future projections.* New York: Free Press.

Chase, Anthony R. 1993. Assessing and addressing problems posed by environmental racism. *Rutgers Law Review* 45(Winter): 335-69.

Commission for Racial Justice. 1987. *Toxic wastes and race in the United States: A national report on the radial and socioeconomic characteristics of communities with hazardous waste sites.* New York: United Church of Christ.

Commission for Racial Justice. 1991. *Program guide: The First National People of Color Environmental Leadership Summit.* New York: United Church of Christ.

Deane, Margaret, Shanna H. Swan, John A. Harris, David M. Epstein, and Raymond R. Neutra. 1989. Adverse pregnancy outcomes in relation to water contamination, Santa Clara County, California, 1980-1981. *American Journal of Epidemiology* 125(5): 894-904.

Environmental Institute, 1992. *Environmental services directory.* Minneapolis, MN: Environmental Information Ltd.

Environmental Protection Agency (EPA), 1992. *Environmental equity: Reducing risk for all communities.* Draft. Washington, DC: Environmental Protection Agency.

General Accounting Office (GAO). 1983. *Siting of hazardous waste landfills and their correlation with racial and economic status of surrounding communities.* Washington, DC: U.S. Government Printing Office.

Geschwind, Sandra A. 1992. Should pregnant women move? Linking risks for birth defects with proximity to toxic waste sites. *Chance* 5:40-45, 86.

Geschwind, Sandra A., Jan A. J. Stolwijk, Michael Bracken, Edward Fitzgerald, Alice Stark, Carolyn Olsen, and James Melius. 1992. Risk of congenital malformations associated with proximity to hazardous waste sites. *American Journal of Epidemiology* 135(11): 1197-1207.

Grisham, Joe W. 1986. *Health aspects of the disposal of waste chemicals.* New York: Pergamon.

Grossfield, Stan. 193. Life in the poison zones. *Boston Sunday Globe*, March 18, A1.

Lazarus, Richard J. 1993. Pursuing "environmental justice": The distributive effects of environmental protection. *Northwestern University Law Review* 57(3): 787-857.

Mohai, Paul, and Bunyan Bryant. 1992. Environmental racism: Reviewing the evidence. In *Race and the incidence of environmental hazards: A time for discourse*, edited by B. Bryant and P. Mohai. Boulder, CO: Westview.

Stephens, Robert D. 1981. Experimental design for wastesite investigation. In *Assessment of health effects at chemical disposal sites*, edited by William W. Lowrance. New York: Rockefeller University.

Swan, Shanna H., Gary Shaw, John A. Harris, and Raymond R. Neutra. 1989. Congenital cardiac anomalies in relation to water contamination, Santa Clara County, California, 1981-1983. *American Journal of Epidemiology* 129(5): 885-93.

U.S. Bureau of the Census. 1980. *Census of population and housing, 1980 (United States): Summary tape file 3.* Washington, DC: U.S. Department of Commerce, Bureau of the Census.

# 3

# Market Forces, Not Racist Practices, May Affect the Siting of Locally Undesirable Land Uses

Vicki Been

*Vicki Been is associate professor of law at New York University School of Law.*

Several studies have shown that a disproportionate number of waste facilities have been sited in minority and poor communities. But these examinations have been based on the *current* socioeconomic makeup of those neighborhoods, which leaves open the possibility that market forces drove down property values in these communities *after* the waste facilities were sited there, thereby attracting the poor and minorities, who are relegated to less desirable neighborhoods through housing discrimination and economic restraints. To close the gap in existing research, two studies were extended from the actual date of siting toward the present. Although the results are mixed, these study extensions show the need for further research into environmental justice. If market forces contribute to the disproportionate siting of polluting facilities in poor and minority neighborhoods, any solutions that do not take these forces into account will be only temporarily effective, at best.

The environmental justice movement contends that people of color and the poor are exposed to greater environmental risks than are whites and wealthier individuals. The movement charges that this disparity is due in part to racism and classism in the siting of environmental risks, the promulgation of environmental laws and regulations, the enforcement of environmental laws, and the attention given to the cleanup of polluted areas.[1] To support the first charge—that the siting of waste dumps, polluting factories, and other locally undesirable land uses (LULUs) had been racist and classist—advocates for environmental justice

Vicki Been, "Locally Undesirable Land Uses in Minority Neighborhoods." Reprinted by permission of The Yale Law Journal Company and Fred B. Rothman & Company from *The Yale Law Journal*, vol. 103, pages 1383-1422.

have cited more than a dozen studies analyzing the relationship between neighborhoods' socioeconomic characteristics and the number of LULUs they host. The studies demonstrate that those neighborhoods in which LULUs are located have, on average, a higher percentage of racial minorities and are poorer than non-host communities.[2]

That research does not, however, establish that the host communities were disproportionately minority or poor at the time the sites were selected. Most of the studies compare the *current* socioeconomic characteristics of communities that host various LULUs to those of communities that do not host such LULUs. This approach leaves open the possibility that the sites for LULUs were chosen fairly,[3] but that subsequent events produced the current disproportion in the distribution of LULUs. In other words, the research fails to prove environmental justice advocates' claim that the disproportionate burden poor and minority communities now bear in hosting LULUs is the result of racism and classism in the *siting process* itself.[4]

---

*Such factors as poverty . . . and the location of jobs . . . may have led the poor and racial minorities to . . . move to neighborhoods that host LULUs [locally undesirable land uses].*

---

In addition, the research fails to explore an alternative or additional explanation for the proven demographics of communities and the likelihood that they host LULUs.[5] Regardless of whether the LULUs originally were sited fairly, it could well be that neighborhoods surrounding LULUs became poorer and became home to a greater percentage of people of color over the years following the sitings. Such factors as poverty, housing discrimination, and the location of jobs, transportation, and other public services may have led the poor and racial minorities to "come to the nuisance"—to move to neighborhoods that host LULUs—because those neighborhoods offered the cheapest available housing. Despite the plausibility of that scenario, none of the existing research on environmental justice has examined how the siting of undesirable land uses has subsequently affected the socioeconomic characteristics of host communities.[6] Because the research fails to prove that the siting process causes any of the disproportionate burden the poor and minorities now bear, and because the research has ignored the possibility that market dynamics may have played some role in the distribution of that burden, policymakers now have no way of knowing whether the siting process is "broke" and needs fixing.[7] Nor can they know whether even an ideal siting system that ensured a perfectly fair initial distribution of LULUs would result in any long-term benefit to the poor or to people of color.

This viewpoint begins to address both of these gaps in the research. Part I of this viewpoint explains how market dynamics may affect the demographics of the communities hosting LULUs. It then demonstrates why an empirical understanding of the role market dynamics play in the distribution is necessary both to focus discussion about the fairness of the existing distribution of LULUs and to fashion an effective remedy for any unfairness in that distribution.

Part II surveys the existing research and explains why it is insufficient to determine whether the siting process placed LULUs in neighborhoods that were disproportionately minority or poor at the time the facility was opened, whether the siting of the facility subsequently drove host neighborhoods to become home to a larger percentage of people of color or the poor than other communities, or whether both of these phenomena contributed to the current distribution of LULUs.

Part III undertakes empirical research to study the roles that initial siting decisions and market dynamics play in the distribution of LULUs. The research extends two of the studies most often cited as proof of environmental racism—the General Accounting Office's *Siting of Hazardous Waste Landfills and Their Correlation with Racial and Economic Status of Surrounding Communities*[8] and Robert Bullard's *Solid Waste Sites and the Black Houston Community*[9]—by analyzing data about the demographic characteristics of host neighborhoods in those studies at the time the siting decisions were made, then tracing demographic changes in the neighborhoods after the siting.

The larger of the two extended studies indicates that market dynamics may play a significant role in creating the disparity between the racial composition of host communities and that of non-host communities.[10] In that sample, LULUs initially were sited somewhat disproportionately in poor communities and communities of color.[11] After the sitings, the levels of poverty and percentages of African-Americans in the host neighborhoods increased, and the property values in these neighborhoods declined. Accordingly, the study suggests that while siting decisions do disproportionately affect minorities and the poor, market dynamics also play a very significant role in creating the uneven distribution of the burdens LULUs impose. Even if siting processes can be improved, therefore, market forces are likely to create a pattern in which LULUs become surrounded by people of color or the poor, and consequently come to impose a disproportionate burden upon those groups. The smaller study, on the other hand, finds a correlation between neighborhood demographics and initial siting decisions, but finds no evidence that market dynamics are leading the poor or people of color to "come to the nuisance."

Like the original studies, the extensions involve samples too small to establish conclusively the cause of disproportionate siting. The extensions are valuable nonetheless because they reveal the gaps in the existing research, improve upon the methodology of the research, and demonstrate that further study of the demographics of host communities at the time their LULUs were sited is likely to produce helpful information about the causes of, and potential solutions for, environmental injustice.[12]

## I. Market dynamics and the distribution of LULUs

The residential housing market in the United States is extremely dynamic. Every year, approximately 17% to 20% of U.S. households move to a new home.[13] Some of those people stay within the same neighborhood, but many move to different neighborhoods in the same city, or to different cities.[14] Some people decide to move, at least in part, because they are dissatisfied with the quality of their current neighborhoods.[15] Once a household decides to move, its choice of a new neighborhood usually depends somewhat on the cost of housing and the characteristics of the neighborhood.[16] Those two factors are interrelated because the quality of the neighborhood affects the price of housing.[17]

The siting of a LULU can influence the characteristics of the surrounding neighborhood in two ways. First, an undesirable land use may cause those who can afford to move to become dissatisfied and leave the neighborhood.[18] Second, by making the neighborhood less desirable, the LULU may decrease the value of the neighborhood's property,[19] making the housing more available to lower income households and less attractive to higher income households.[20] The end result of both influences is likely to be that the neighborhood becomes poorer than it was before the siting of the LULU.

The neighborhood also is likely to become home to more people of color. Racial discrimination in the sale and rental of housing relegates people of color (especially African-Americans) to the least desirable neighborhoods, regardless of their income level.[21] Moreover, once a neighborhood becomes a community of color, racial discrimination in the promulgation and enforcement of zoning and environmental protection laws,[22] the provision of municipal services,[23] and the lending practices of banks[24] may cause neighborhood quality to decline further.[25] That additional decline, in turn, will induce those who can leave the neighborhood—the least poor and those least subject to discrimination—to do so.

The dynamics of the housing market therefore are likely to cause the poor and people of color to move to or remain in the neighborhoods in which LULUs are located, regardless of the demographics of the communities when the LULUs were first sited. As long as the market allows the existing distribution of wealth to allocate goods and services, it would be surprising indeed if, over the long run, LULUs did not impose a disproportionate burden upon the poor. And as long as the market discriminates on the basis of race, it would be remarkable if LULUs did not eventually impose a disproportionate burden upon people of color.

---

*Even if siting processes can be improved . . . market forces are likely to create a pattern in which LULUs become surrounded by people of color or the poor.*

---

By failing to address how LULUs have affected the demographics of their host communities, the current research has ignored the possibility that the correlation between the location of LULUs and the socioeconomic characteristics of neighborhoods may be a function of aspects of our free market system other than, or in addition to, the siting process. It is crucial to examine that possibility. Both the justice of the distribution of LULUs and the remedy for any injustice may differ if market dynamics play a significant role in the distribution.

If the siting process is primarily responsible for the correlation between the location of LULUs and the demographics of host neighborhoods, the process may be unjust under current constitutional doctrine, at least as to people of color. Siting processes that result in the selection of host neighborhoods that are disproportionately poor (but not disproportionately composed of people of color) would not be unconstitutional because the Supreme Court has been reluctant to recognize poverty as a suspect classification.[26] A siting process motivated by racial prejudice, however, would be unconstitutional.[27] A process that disproportionately affects people of color[28] also would be unfair under some statutory schemes and some constitutional theories of discrimination.[29]

On the other hand, if the disproportionate distribution of LULUs results from market forces which drive the poor, regardless of their race,[30] to live in neighborhoods that offer cheaper housing because they host LULUs, then the fairness of the distribution becomes a question about the fairness of our market economy. Some might argue that the disproportionate burden is part and parcel of a free market economy that is, overall, fairer than alternative schemes, and that the costs of regulating the market to reduce the disproportionate burden outweigh the benefits of doing so. Others might argue that those moving to a host neighborhood are compensated through the market for the disproportionate burden they bear by lower housing costs, and therefore that the situation is just. Similarly, some might contend that while the poor suffer lower quality neighborhoods, they also suffer lower quality food, housing, and medical care, and that the systemic problem of poverty is better addressed through income redistribution programs than through changes in siting processes.

Even if decisionmakers were to agree that it is unfair to allow post-siting market dynamics to create disproportionate environmental risk for the poor or minorities, the remedy for that injustice would have to be much more fundamental than the remedy for unjust siting *decisions*. Indeed, if market forces are the primary cause of the correlation between the presence of LULUs and the current socioeconomic characteristics of a neighborhood, even a siting process radically revised to ensure that LULUs are distributed equally among all neighborhoods may have only a short-term effect.[31] The areas surrounding LULUs distributed equitably will become less desirable neighborhoods, and thus may soon be left to people of color or the poor, recreating the pattern of inequitable siting. Accordingly, if a disproportionate burden results from or is exacerbated by market dynamics, an effective remedy might require such reforms as stricter enforcement of laws against housing discrimination, more serious efforts to achieve residential integration, changes in the processes of siting low and moderate income housing, changes in programs designed to aid the poor in securing decent housing, greater regulatory protection for those neighborhoods that are chosen to host LULUs, and changes in production and consumption processes to reduce the number of LULUs needed.

Information about the role market dynamics play in the distribution of LULUs would promote a better understanding of the nature of the problem of environmental injustice and help point the way to appropriate solutions for the problem. Nonetheless, market dynamics have been largely ignored by the current research on environmental justice.

## II. The evidence of disproportionate siting

Several recent studies have attempted to assess whether locally undesirable land uses are disproportionately located[32] in neighborhoods that are populated by more people of color or are more poor than is normal. The most important of the studies was published in 1987 by the United Church of Christ Commission for Racial Justice (CRJ).[33] The CRJ conducted a cross-sectional study of the racial and socioeconomic characteristics of residents of the zip code areas surrounding 415 commercial hazardous waste facilities[34] and compared those characteristics to those of zip code areas which did not have such facilities.[35] The study revealed a correlation between the number of commercial hazardous waste facilities[36] in an area and the percentage of the "nonwhite" population in the area.[37] Areas that had one operating commercial hazardous waste facility, other than a landfill, had about twice as many people of color as a percentage of the population as those that had no such facility.[38] Areas that had more than one operating facility, or had one of the five largest landfills, had more than three times the percentage of minority residents as areas that had no such facilities.[39]

Several regional and local studies buttress the findings of the nationwide CRJ study.[40] The most frequently cited of those studies, which is often credited for first giving the issue of environmental justice visibility, was conducted by the United States General Accounting Office (GAO). The GAO examined the racial and socioeconomic characteristics of the communities surrounding four hazardous waste landfills in the eight southeastern states that make up EPA's Region IV.[41] The sites studied include some of the largest landfills in the United States. . . .

[The GAO found that] three of the four communities where such landfills were sited were majority African-American in 1980; African-Americans made up 52%, 66%, and 90% of the population in those three communities.[42] In contrast, African-Americans made up between 22% and 30% of the host states' populations.[43] The host communities were all disproportionately poor, with between 26% and 42% of the population living below the poverty level.[44] In comparison, the host states' poverty rates ranged from 14% to 19%.[45]

Another frequently cited local study was conducted by sociologist Robert Bullard[46] and formed important parts of his books, *Invisible Houston*[47] and *Dumping in Dixie*.[48] Professor Bullard found that although African-Americans made up only 28% of the Houston population in 1980, six of Houston's eight incinerators and mini-incinerators and fifteen of seventeen landfills were located in predominantly African-American neighborhoods.[49]

With one exception, described below, none of the existing studies addressed the question of which came first—the people of color and the poor, or the LULU.[50] As noted by the CRJ, the studies "were not designed to show cause and effect,"[51] but only to explore the relationship between the current distribution of LULUs and host communities' demographics. The evidence of disproportionate siting is thus incomplete: it does not establish that *the siting process* had a disproportionate effect upon minorities or the poor.

Professor James T. Hamilton of Duke University has performed the only research to date that has addressed the "which came first" question. Professor Hamilton recently examined how the planned capacity changes for hazardous waste processing facilities in 1987 correlated with the political power (measured by voter registration) of the facilities' host counties as of the 1980 census.[52] In the course of his study, Professor Hamilton also examined correlations between planned capacity changes and county demographics. Because Professor Hamilton's analysis examined decisions about whether to expand or contract facilities that were made five or six years after the census from which data on the county's socioeconomic characteristics were derived, and because decisions to expand or contract capacity share some of the same characteristics as initial siting decisions,[53] his analysis is probative of whether there is a correlation between siting decisions and the characteristics of affected communities near the time of those decisions. Professor Hamilton concluded that when other factors were controlled, the race and income of the county at the time of the expansion decisions were not significant predictors of expansion plans.[54] Race was a statistically significant determinant of the facilities' plans to reduce capacity, however; as the percentage of a county's minority population increased, it was less likely that the facility planned to reduce its capacity.[55]

---

*Others might argue that those moving to a host neighborhood are compensated through the market for the disproportionate burden they bear by lower housing costs.*

---

In addition, Professor Hamilton compared 1970 census data regarding the counties in which surveyed facilities were sited in the 1970's and early 1980's to census data for all counties in the United States. Professor Hamilton found that both race and median household income were statistically significant predictors of sitings during the 1970's and early 1980's.[56] Professor Hamilton's study has several limitations: the sample did not include facilities that went out of business before the 1987 survey;[57] the data examined was for entire counties rather than the tracts or county subdivisions in which the facility was actually located;[58] and the 1970 census data was used even for siting decisions made in the early 1980's.[59] The study nevertheless provides important evidence that the siting process itself has had a disproportionate effect on low income communities and communities of color. Professor Hamilton did not examine whether the socioeconomic characteristics of host communities changed once the facilities were sited, however, so his study does not provide any evidence about the role that market dynamics may play in the distribution of LULUs.

In summary, with the exception of Professor Hamilton's study, the existing research fails to focus on the characteristics of communities at the time LULUs were sited, and therefore cannot establish whether the correlation between a neighborhood's current demographics and the number of LULUs it hosts was caused by the siting process. None of the existing research examines how market dynamics affected the socioeconomic characteristics of host neighborhoods. The literature therefore sheds little light on whether the current distribution of LULUs resulted from siting processes that had a disproportionate effect upon minorities and the poor, or from market dynamics, or both.

## III. The effects of siting practices and market dynamics

To begin to fill the gaps in the literature, this Part expands the GAO and Bullard studies described above. First, it adds to those studies data regarding the socioeconomic characteristics of the host communities at the time the siting decisions were made. Second, it traces changes in the demographics of the host communities since the sitings took place.

*A. The GAO study*

Of the four hazardous waste landfills studied by the GAO, one became operational in 1972, two in 1977, and one in 1979.[60] The process of choosing a site, applying for the necessary permits, and constructing the landfill typically takes at least several years, so it is likely that the sites for the three landfills that became operational in 1972 and 1977 were chosen in the early or mid-1970's.[61] One would therefore learn more about whether those siting choices had a disproportionate effect on the poor or people of color by examining the socioeconomic characteristics of those three communities in 1970, rather than 1980.[62]

The 1970 data for those three sites and the 1980 data for the remaining site reveal that all of the host communities were disproportionately populated by African-Americans at the time of the sitings. The percentage of the host communities' populations that was African-American ranged from 1.6 times to 3.3 times that of the host states' populations.[63] Accordingly, demographic data from the time of the siting supports the inference that the siting process was flawed in a way that caused siting choices to have a disproportionate effect upon people of color.

Conversely, the data provide no support for the theory that market dynamics will cause host neighborhoods to become increasingly populated by people of color. In each of the four communities the GAO studied, the siting of the landfill was followed by a decrease in the percentage of the community that was African-American. While the change was insignificant in two of the host communities, the African-American percentage of the population in two of the host communities declined precipitously. The area surrounding the Industrial Chemical Facility in Chester County, South Carolina, had a 35.8% decrease in the percentage of its population that was African-American between 1970 and 1990. Similarly, the area surrounding the SCA Services facility in Sumter County, South Carolina, had a 32.3% decrease between 1970 and 1990. By contrast, South Carolina as a whole had a 2.3% decrease between 1970 and 1990.

The substantial decrease in the percentage of African-American residents in these communities contradicts the theory that a landfill changes the demographics of neighboring areas by making them less attractive places to live, thereby decreasing property values and rents, and attracting people who are unable to afford other neighborhoods, or who are excluded from other neighborhoods by racial discrimination.[64] The theory is further undermined by the remaining evidence. The relative poverty[65] and relative median family income of the host counties changed only marginally[66] between 1970 and 1990.[67] Further, the relative median housing value changed only slightly between 1970 and 1990, and, in two of the four host communities, the relative median housing value increased. If the market dynamics theory were correct, the data should show decreases in relative median family income and relative median housing values and increases in relative poverty over the decades after the siting.

In sum, an examination of the characteristics of the host communities at issue in the GAO study at the time the facilities were sited shows that the host communities were home to a considerably larger percentage of African-Americans and were somewhat poorer than other communities within the host states. The analysis therefore suggests that the siting process had a disproportionate effect on the poor and people of color. At the same time, the analysis provides no support for the theory that the location of LULUs in poor or minority communities is a result of the dynamics of the housing market.

*B. The Bullard study*

The second part of this study uses a subgroup of the sites that were the subject of Professor Bullard's 1983 study of the location of incinerators and landfills in Houston. Professor Bullard's study concluded that twenty-one of Houston's twenty-five incinerators, mini-incinerators and landfills were located in predominantly African-American neighborhoods.[68]

---

*None of the existing studies addressed the question of which came first—the people of color and the poor, or the LULU.*

---

The extension of Professor Bullard's study presented here eliminates data about Houston's unpermitted municipal landfills and incinerators from the sample. Those landfills and incinerators were sited as long ago as 1920, and all had ceased to operate by the 1970's. Because census tracts were quite large during the early decades of the century, it is impossible to evaluate in any meaningful way the racial and class characteristics of communities chosen to host LULUs that long ago. In addition, the revision collapses the categories that Professor Bullard differentiated as "Browning Ferris Industries Landfill Sites" and "Texas Department of Health Permitted Municipal Landfill Sites"[69] because three of the landfills fall into both categories, and were essentially "double-counted" in Professor Bullard's study.[70] To avoid double-counting, the revision also combines what Professor Bullard lists separately as the American Refuse Systems and Browning Ferris Industries sites, because those sites are in fact the same landfill.[71] Of what Professor Bullard lists as twenty-five sites, then, the revision looks at three mini-incinerators and seven landfills.

There is another important difference between the extension and Professor Bullard's original analysis. While Professor Bullard's published accounts of his study do not explain his methodology, Professor Bullard has explained in correspondence that his study did not use census tracts as its unit of analysis, but instead used "neighborhoods."[72] In contrast, this extension examines census tract data. Professor Bullard's published accounts of his study do not provide information about how he defined the neighborhoods surrounding the sites, and it therefore is impossible to replicate his analysis on a neighborhood basis.

In addition, there are significant advantages to using census tracts rather than smaller "neighborhoods" as the unit of analysis for examining the distribution of undesirable land uses.[73] The advantage of neighborhood units of analysis, such as blocks or block groups, is that such data are less likely to hide differences in the population within the unit.[74] The disadvantages of such small units of analysis, however, are substantial. Although a facility may have its most immediate impact on the few blocks immediately contiguous to the facility, there is substantial reason to doubt that the impact stops there.[75] In addition, data often are not available for finer units of analysis, because where a block is so small that the confidentiality of the census survey respondents would be compromised by release of the data, the Census Bureau suppresses the data.[76] Blocks vary greatly in area and density, so comparisons based on block and block group data will be misleading unless adjusted for differences in the size of the population.[77] Finally, block groups change in configuration over time, so problems occur in comparing data across decades.[78]

Census tracts, on the other hand, are structured to be relatively permanent.[79] They are supposed to have between 2500 and 8000 people each, so they can be compared without adjustments for area or density.[80] Tracts comprehensively cover almost all metropolitan populations.[81] When formed, census tracts are supposed to be as homogenous as possible.[82] Because of these advantages, census tracts often are used as the unit of analysis in studying a "neighborhood."[83] Indeed, almost all of the literature on the siting of undesirable land uses described in Part II uses census tracts or larger census units as the unit of analysis; none uses blocks or block grouping.[84]

Of the ten sites used in the revision, all the mini-incinerators and four of the landfills were sited in the early 1970's, so 1970 census data is most relevant for those sites. Two adjacent landfills were sited in the early and mid-1950's; for those sites, 1960 data was also analyzed (the tract in which the landfills were located was so large in 1950 that the 1950 data is not comparable to the later data). The remaining landfill was permitted in 1978; because that siting decision was most likely made after 1975, the 1980 census data is most relevant for that site.

[Census data] reveal that, of the seven landfills sited between 1953 and 1978, four host neighborhoods had about the same or a lower percentage of African-Americans in their populations than Houston as a whole, while three had percentages above Houston's. Of the mini-incinerators sited in 1972, one was sited in an almost all-white neighborhood, and the other two were sited in neighborhoods with substantially more African-Americans as a percentage of their populations than Houston as a whole. Accordingly, three of the seven landfills and two of the three mini-incinerators (or half of all the facilities) were sited in areas that were disproportionately African-American at the time of the siting. About one-quarter of Houston's population was African-American during the relevant decades. Thus, the fact that one-half the sites were in neighborhoods that had more African-Americans as a percentage of their population than did Houston as a whole indicates that the siting process had some disproportionate effect.[85]

Analysis of the neighborhoods' demographics in the decades after the LULUs were sited, however, reveals that the siting process was not the sole cause of the disproportionate burden that African-American communities now bear. The number of African-Americans as a percentage of the population increased between 1970 and 1980 in all the neighborhoods surrounding the landfills. That increase was by as much as 223%, compared to a 7% increase in the African-American population of Houston as a whole. As a result, by the 1980 census, four of the seven neighborhoods hosting landfills and two of three neighborhoods hosting mini-incinerators had a greater percentage of African-Americans in their populations than Houston as a whole.

This trend continued between 1980 and 1990. In all but one neighborhood, the percentage of African-Americans continued to increase, even though the percentage of African-Americans in Houston as a whole stayed constant. The increases were less dramatic than the changes between 1970 and 1980, with all but two of the neighborhoods increasing by less than 10%. The end result, however, was that by the 1990 census, all of the neighborhoods hosting landfills had become home to a disproportionate percentage of African-Americans.

Examination of the host neighborhoods' economic characteristics reveals a similar pattern. Only two of the seven areas hosting landfills and one of the three areas hosting mini-incinerators had poverty rates significantly higher than Harris County's [Houston] at the time their facilities were sited.[86] The percentage of the host neighborhoods' populations with income under the poverty level increased between 1970 and 1980, however, in all but two of the host neighborhoods, even though Harris County's poverty rate dropped. Between 1980 and 1990, four of the seven neighborhoods hosting landfills had increases in their poverty rates that were significantly higher than the increases in poverty suffered by Harris County. As a result, by the time of the 1990 census, five of the seven areas hosting landfills and two of the three areas hosting mini-incinerators had become significantly poorer than Harris County.

Median family incomes in all but one of the neighborhoods surrounding landfills also lost ground relative to Harris County between 1970 and 1980, and further worsened between 1980 and 1990. In addition, all but one of the host communities where landfills[87] were sited before 1972 suffered marked declines in their housing values relative to Harris County over the decades following the sitings.[88]

In sum, examining the data for the census closest to the date of each siting decision shows that the siting process had a disproportionate effect upon African-Americans. In addition, such an analysis provides considerable support for the theory that market dynamics contribute to the disproportionate burden LULUs impose upon people of color and the poor. As the argument that LULUs change a neighborhood's demographics by driving down property values would predict, the data reveal that the homes surrounding the landfill sites in most of the host neighborhoods became less valuable properties relative to other areas of Harris County after the landfills were sited, and the host communities became increasingly populated by African-Americans and increasingly poor.

The extensions of the GAO and Bullard studies, as well as Professor Hamilton's study of facilities' expansion and reduction plans, show the effect of using demographic data from the census closest to the actual siting or capacity change decision (rather than the latest census data). Tracing changes in the demographics from this baseline reveals a significant difference in the evidence the studies provide regarding the burden LULUs impose on minorities and the poor. These studies suggest that the siting process bears some responsibility for the disproportionate burden waste facilities now impose upon the poor and people of color.[89] The extension of the GAO study suggests that market dynamics play no role in the distribution of the burden. The extension of the Bullard study, on the other hand, suggests that market dynamics do play a significant role in that distribution.

The different results obtained by the two extensions may be attributable to the generally slower rate of residential mobility in rural areas, such as those hosting the GAO sites, versus urban areas, such as those hosting the Houston sites.[90] The difference also may be attributable to the size and nature of the facilities studied in the two extensions. The sites studied in the GAO report are quite large, and provide a substantial number of jobs to residents of the host counties.[91] Persons moving to the area to take those jobs may have displaced the African-Americans who previously lived in the community. The sites at issue in Professor Bullard's study, on the other hand, were unlikely to have created many new jobs, and those jobs that were created would have been much less likely than the jobs at the GAO sites to induce people to move nearby in order to take them.

Significant evidence suggests that LULUs are disproportionately located in neighborhoods that are now home to more of the nation's people of color and poor than other neighborhoods. Efforts to address that disparity are hampered, however, by the lack of data about which came first—the people of color and poor or the LULU. If the neighborhoods were disproportionately populated by people of color or the poor at the time the siting decisions were made, a reasonable inference can be drawn that the siting process had a disproportionate effect upon the poor and people of color. In that case, changes in the siting process may be required.

On the other hand, if, after the LULU was built, the neighborhoods in which LULUs were sited became increasingly poor, or became home to an increasing percentage of people of color, the cure for the problem of disproportionate siting is likely to be much more complicated and difficult. The distribution of LULUs would then look more like a confluence of the forces of housing discrimination, poverty, and free market economics. Remedies would have to take those forces into account.

The preliminary evidence derived from this extension of two of the leading studies of environmental justice, along with the evidence offered by Professor Hamilton's study of capacity expansion plans, shows that research examining the socioeconomic characteristics of host neighborhoods at the time they were selected, then tracing changes in those characteristics following the siting, would go a long way toward answering the question of which came first—the LULU or its minority or poor neighbors. Until that research is complete, proposed "solutions" to the problem of disproportionate siting run a substantial risk of missing the mark.

## Notes

1. *See, e.g.,* ROBERT D. BULLARD, DUMPING IN DIXIE: RACE, CLASS, AND ENVIRONMENTAL QUALITY 1-6 (1990); Robert D. Bullard, *The Threat of Environmental Racism,* 7 NAT. RESOURCES & ENV'T 23 (1993); Luke W.Cole, *Empowerment as the Key to Environmental Protection: The Need for Environmental Poverty Law,* 19 ECOLOGY L.Q. 619, 629-30 (1992); Karl Grossman, *Environmental Justice,* E MAG., May-June 1992, at 29,31.

2. *See infra* text accompanying notes 32-59. The literature seems to assume that a siting pattern is disproportionate whenever the percentage of people of color in a host community is higher than the percentage of people of color in the nation's population or in the population of non-host communities. This measure of proportionality is simplistic. First, it ignores the density of population within a neighborhood. *Cf.* Michael Greenberg, *Proving Environmental Inequity in Siting Locally Unwanted Land Uses,* 4 RISK: ISSUES IN HEALTH & SAFETY 235, 244-49 (1993) (showing how use of statistics weighted by population of communities studied affects analysis of inequity). Assume, for example, that a siting decisonmaker is faced with two communities, one of which has 5000 people, 12% of whom are people of color, while the other has 1000 people, 20% of whom are people of color. Assume also that the percentage of people of color in the nation is 12%. Under the measure of proportionality generally used in the literature, the LULU would be disproportionately sited if it were placed in the second community, even though that choice would expose fewer people of color to the LULU than would the other site. A better measure of proportionality would take into account the number of people affected by a siting, rather than just focusing on the percentage of the affected population that is composed of people of color. *Cf.* UNITED CHURCH OF CHRIST COMM'N FOR RACIAL JUSTICE, TOXIC WASTES AND RACE IN THE UNITED STATES 53 (1987) [hereinafter CRJ REPORT] (finding that the percentage of people of color living in communities with uncontrolled toxic waste sites—56.32%—was only slightly higher than the percentage of

whites living in such communities—53.60%). Second, this measure of proportionality can be misleading if studies do not provide information about how far the distribution of the population within the host neighborhoods deviates from the national distribution. By describing a community as "minority" or "poor" whenever the percentage of people of color or poor in the community exceeds that of the population as a whole, a study using this measure of proportionality could classify a LULU as disproportionately sited even if it is located in a predominantly white neighborhood in which the population variance from the national distribution is statistically insignificant. *Compare* CRJ, *supra*, at 41 (providing information about degree of variance between the distribution of the population in host and non-host communities) *with* the studies discussed *infra* text accompanying notes 41-49 (failing to provide such information).

3. What it means to site LULUs "fairly" is a complex and controversial issue. For a full discussion of that issue, see Vicki Been, *What's Fairness Got To Do with It? Environmental Justice and the Siting of Locally Undesirable Land Uses*, 78 CORNELL L. REV. 1001 (1993). For the purposes of this discussion, a "fair" siting will be considered one that has no disproportionate effect upon the poor or upon people of color.

4. Both of the leading studies of siting disparities recognize that analysis of the current demographics of host communities does not establish that discrimination in the siting process caused any of the disproportionate burden those communities now bear. *See* U.S. GEN. ACCOUNTING OFFICE, GAO/RCED-83-168, SITING OF HAZARDOUS WASTE LAND-FILLS AND THEIR CORRELATION WITH RACIAL AND ECONOMIC STATUS OF SURROUNDING COMMUNITIES 3 (1983) [hereinafter GAO REPORT]; CRJ REPORT, *supra* note 2, at 11. For discussions of how existing studies fail to prove causation, see Been, *supra* note 3, at 1016-18; Michael B. Gerrard, *Fear and Loathing in the Siting of Hazardous and Radioactive Waste Facilities: A Comprehensive Approach to a Misperceived Crisis*, 68 TUL. L. REV. (forthcoming 1994) (manuscript at 125, 132, on file with author); James T. Hamilton, *Politics and Social Costs: Estimating the impact of Collective Action on Hazardous Waste Facilities*, 24 RAND J. ECON. 101, 110 (1993); Richard J. Lazarus, *Pursuing "Environmental Justice": The Distributional Effects of Environmental Protection*, 87 NW. U. L. REV. 787, 802 n.56 (1993). *Cf.* Bean v. Southwestern Waste Management Corp., 482 F. Supp. 673, 677 (S. D. Tex. 1979) (holding that to establish a pattern or practice of discriminatory siting, data must show demographics of host communities "on the day that the sites opened"), *aff'd* 782 F.2d 1038 (5th Cir. 1986).

5. While this Article focuses on market dynamics as an alternative explanation for the correlation, other potential explanations should be explored as well. For example, siting decisionmakers may seek to distribute sites fairly but face constraints imposed by regulations over which they have no control, such as zoning regulations. Those zoning regulations may underprotect the interests of the poor or people of color. *See* Jon C. Dubin, *From Junkyards to Gentrification: Explicating a Right to Protective Zoning in Low-Income Communities of Color*, 77 MINN. L. REV. 739 (1993); Yale Rabin, *Expulsive Zoning: The Inequitable Legacy of* Euclid, *in* ZONING AND THE AMERICAN DREAM 101 (Charles M. Haar & Jerold S. Kayden eds., 1989).

6. A few studies, ignored by the environmental justice literature, have examined the effects various land uses have had on neighboring property values, turnover within a neighborhood, and the socioeconomic characteristics of the neighborhood. *See, e.g.*, MENTAL HEALTH LAW PROJECT, THE EFFECTS OF GROUP HOMES ON NEIGHBORING PROPERTY; AN ANNOTATED BIBLIOGRAPHY 1-15 (1988) (surveying the literature on the effects community residential facilities have on property values and neighborhood turnover); U.S. GEN. ACCOUNTING OFFICE, GAO/HRD-83-14, AN ANALYSIS OF ZONING AND OTHER PROBLEMS AFFECTING THE ESTABLISHMENT OF GROUP HOMES FOR THE MENTALLY DISABLED app. III at 62 (1983) (reporting results of survey of turnover and demographic change in neighborhoods hosting group homes); Diana A. Arens, *What Do the Neighbors Think Now? Community Residences on Long Island, New York*, 29 COMMUNITY MENTAL HEALTH J. 235 (1993) (finding that group homes for mentally ill adults have no adverse effects on property values); Michael Dear, *Impact of Mental Health Facilities on Property Values*, 13 COMMUNITY MENTAL HEALTH J. 150 (1977) (discussing housing turnover and property values following opening of group homes). Those studies, however, do not focus on how market dynamics affect the distribution of group homes.

7. Nevertheless, Congress is now considering several bills intended to "correct" the siting process. *See, e.g.*, Environmental Justice Act of 1992, H.R. 2105, 103d Cong., 1st Sess. (1993); Environmental Equal Rights Act of 1993, H.R. 1924, 103d Cong., 1st Sess. (1993); S. 533, 103d Cong., 1st Sess. (1993). State legislatures are considering similar

proposals. *See, e.g.*, Cal. A.B. 2212, 1993-94 Reg. Sess. (1993); N.Y. S.B. 5742, 1993-94 Reg. Sess. (1993).

8. GAO REPORT, *supra* note 4.

9. Robert D. Bullard, *Solid Waste Sites and the Black Houston Community*, 53 SOC. IN-QUIRY 273 (1983) [hereinafter Bullard, *Solid Waste*].

10. *See infra* text accompanying notes 85-88.

11. The sitings had a disproportionate effect in that host neighborhoods had a higher percentage of African-Americans and the poor than non-host neighborhoods. For criticism of that measure of proportionality, see *supra* note 2.

12. On basis of the research reported here, the author has received an exploratory research grant from the U.S Environmental Protection Agency (EPA) to pursue further research on the role market dynamics play in the distribution of the burdens LULUs impose. That study will analyze the socioeconomic characteristics of neighborhoods hosting various LULUs as of the census closest to the date of the relevant siting decision. The study will then trace changes in the neighborhoods' demographic characteristics after the LULUs were constructed. The study will focus on those communities that host hazardous waste treatment, disposal, and storage facilities regulated under the Resource Conservation and Recovery Act, 42 U.S.C. §§ 6901-6987 (1988), as well as those that host the toxic waste sites included on the EPA's National Priorities List for cleanup under the Comprehensive Environmental Response, Compensation, and Liability Act, 42 U.S.C. §§ 9601-9675 (1988).

13. BUREAU OF THE CENSUS, U.S. DEP'T OF COMMERCE, CURRENT POPULATION REPORTS, SERIES P-20 No. 463, GEOGRAPHICAL MOBILITY: MARCH 1990 TO MARCH 1991 VIII (1992) [hereinafter GEOGRAPHICAL MOBILITY]. The figures given are for the period between 1970 and 1991. *Id.* In the Houston area, which is the subject of one of the extended studies reported in Part III, *infra*, only 45% of the population five years old or older lived in 1990 in the same house they had lived in five years earlier. BUREAU OF THE CENSUS, U.S. DEP'T OF COMMERCE, 1990 CPH-3-176B, 1990 CENSUS OF POPULATION AND HOUSING, POPULATION AND HOUSING CHARACTERISTICS FOR CENSUS TRACTS AND BLOCK NUMBERING AREAS, HOUSTON-GALVESTON-BRAZORIA, TX CMSA (PART) 87 (1993).

14. Between 1970 and 1991, for example, between 6.0% and 6.7% of the population moved each year from the county in which they had been residing. GEOGRAPHICAL MOBILITY, *supra* note 13, at VIII. During the five-year period between 1975 and 1980, 21% of all persons 15 years and over moved between counties, between states, or from abroad. BUREAU OF THE CENSUS, U.S. DEP'T OF COMMERCE, PC 80-2-2A, 1980 CENSUS OF THE POPULATION, GEOGRAPHICAL MOBILITY FOR STATES AND THE NATION 65 (1984).

15. *See, e.g.*, ALDEN SPEARE, JR. ET AL., RESIDENTIAL MOBILITY, MIGRATION, AND METROPOLITAN CHANGE 235-36 (1975); Thomas P. Boehm & Keith R. Ihlanfeldt, *Residential Mobility and Neighborhood Quality*, 26 J. REGIONAL SCI. 411, 419 (1986); John M. Quigley & Daniel H. Weinberg, *Intra-Urban Residential Mobility: A Review and Synthesis*, 2 INT'L REGIONAL SCI. REV. 41, 55-56 (1977) (reviewing the literature). Of course, the location of jobs, the size and composition of the family, and ties to family and friends often are the primary factors in a household's decision to move. *See* Quigley & Weinberg, *supra*, at 49-55.

16. *See, e.g.*, SPEARE ET AL., *supra* note 15, at 236-37; David P. Varady, *Influences on the City-Suburban Choice: A Study of Cincinnati Homebuyers*, 56 J. AM. PLAN. ASS'N 22, 26 (1990).

17. *See, e.g.*, Maureen L. Cropper & Wallace E. Oates, *Environmental Economics: A Survey*, 30 J. ECON. LIT. 675,706-08,717-18 (1992) (surveying the literature); A. Myrick Freeman III, *The Hedonic Price Approach to Measuring Demand for Neighborhood Characteristics*, *in* THE ECONOMICS OF NEIGHBORHOOD 191-92 (David Segal ed., 1979) (reviewing the literature).

18. *See, e.g.*, Mark Baldassare et al., *Urban Service and Environmental Stressor: The Impact of the Bay Area Rapid Transit System (BART) on Residential Mobility*, 11 ENV'T & BEHAV. 435, 441-42 (1979); Quigley & Weinberg, *supra* note 15, at 55-56.

19. The data regarding the impact LULUs have on neighboring property values are inconclusive. Most studies show that hazardous waste sites have a statistically significant adverse impact on the value of surrounding properties. *See* Been, *supra* note 3, at nn. 109-10 (reviewing the literature). For studies not included in that review, see M. Greenberg & Hughes, *The Impact of Hazardous Waste Superfund Sites on the Value of Houses sold in New Jersey*, 26 ANNALS REGIONAL SCI. 147 (1992); Robert Mendelson, et al., *Measuring Hazardous Waste Damages with Panel Models*, 22 J. ENVTL. ECON. & MGMT. 259 (1992). Studies of the effect solid waste landfills and incinerators have on neighboring property

values have reached contradictory conclusions, with slightly more than half showing no effect. Chris Zeiss, *Municipal Solid Waste Incinerator Impacts on Residential Property Values and Sales in Host Communities*, 20 J. ENVTL. SYS. 229, 238-39 (1990-91) (reviewing the literature). Social services LULUs, such as group homes, generally have been shown to have no detrimental impact on neighboring property values. *See* Been *supra* note 3, at 1022-23 & nn. 113-15 (surveying the literature); *see also* sources cited *supra* note 6.

20. To the extent that people choose to stay in a neighborhood, or to move to a different neighborhood, in order to live among others who have similar socioeconomic characteristics, neighborhoods that become poorer because a LULU has decreased property values will begin a spiral in which "households move in response to the changed character of the neighbors[,] . . . the individual decisions of all who move [further] change the character of their neighborhood," more people then leave, and so on. *See* John M. Quigley, *Local Residential Mobility and Local Government Policy*, *in* RESIDENTIAL MOBILITY AND PUBLIC POLICY 39, 45 (W.A.V. Clark & Eric G. Moore eds., 1980) . For evidence that people's decision to move and their choice of neighborhood is influenced by their desire to be near others who are "like me," *see* William M. Dobriner, *Class in Suburbia* 64-67 (1963); Andrew Reschovsky, *Residential Choice and the Local Public Sector: An Alternative Test of the "Tiebout Hypothesis,"* 6 J. URB. ECON. 501, 512 (1979).

21. For discussions of the continuing prevalence of racial discrimination in the housing market, *see, e.g.*, PETER MIESZKOWSKI, STUDIES OF PREJUDICE AND DISCRIMINATION IN URBAN HOUSING MARKETS (1980); John O. Calmore, *To Make Wrong Right: The Necessary and Proper Aspirations of Fair Housing*, *in* THE STATE OF BLACK AMERICA 1989, at 77, 90-95 (Janet Dewart ed., 1989); Dubin, *supra* note 5, at 741 & n. 7, 776 & n. 165. For descriptions of how African-American households are disproportionately located in the poorest of all neighborhoods, *see, e.g.*, Paul A. Jargowsky & Mary J. Bane, *Ghetto Poverty in the United States, 1970-1980*, *in* THE URBAN UNDERCLASS 235, 252 (Christopher Jencks, & Paul E. Peterson eds., 1991); Richard P. Nathan & Charles F. Adams, Jr., *Four Perspectives on Urban Hardship*, 104 POL. SCI. Q. 483, 504 (1989).

22. For discussions of discrimination in the promulgation and enforcement of zoning laws, *see* Dubin, *supra* note 5; Rabin *supra* note 5. For discussions of discrimination in the enforcement of environmental protection laws, *see* Marianne Lavelle & Marcia Coyle, *Unequal Protection: The Racial Divide in Environmental Law*, NAT'L L. J., Sept. 21, 1992, at S2 (finding that "penalties against pollution law violators in minority areas are lower than those imposed for violations in largely white areas, . . . the government takes longer to address hazards in minority communities, and it accepts solutions less stringent than those recommended by the scientific community"); Rae Zimmerman, *Social Equity and Environmental Risk*, 13 RISK ANALYSIS: INT'L J. 649, 660-64, (1993) (finding that the higher the percentage of African-Americans in community, the less likely it was that hazardous waste sites in community had progressed to "Record of Decision" stage of cleanup, especially when community was also relatively poor; but finding that difference was primarily a function of how long site had been listed on National Priorities List). *But see* John A. Hird, *Environmental Policy and Equity: The Case of Superfund*, 12 J. POL'Y ANALYSIS & MGMT. 323, 337 (1993) (finding no relationship between pace at which sites are cleaned up and host county's socioeconomic characteristics).

23. For discussions of discrimination in the provision of municipal services, *see, e.g.*, CHARLES M. HAAR & DANIEL W. FESSLER, THE WRONG SIDE OF THE TRACKS 38-41 (1986); EQUITY IN THE CITY (P.N. Troy ed., 1981); ROBERT L. LINEBERRY, EQUALITY AND URBAN POLICY (1977); Kenneth W. Bond, *Toward Equal Delivery of Municipal Services in the Central Cities*, 4 FORDHAM URB. L. J. 263 (1976); Robert L. Graham & Jason H. Kravitt, *The Evolution of Equal Protection—Education, Municipal Services and Wealth*, 7 HARV. C.R.-C.L. L. REV. 103, 111, 154-68 (1972); Robert P. Inman & Daniel L. Rubinfeld, *The Judicial Pursuit of Local Fiscal Equity*, 92 HARV. L. REV. 1662, 1697-1701 (1979); Peter A. Lupsha & William J. Siembieda, *The Poverty of Public Services In the Land of Plenty*, *in* THE RISE OF THE SUNBELT CITIES 169, 183 (David C. Perry & Alfred J. Watkins eds., 1977); Gershon M. Ratner, *Inter-Neighborhood Denials of Equal Protection in the Provision of Municipal Services*, 4 HAR. C.R.-C.L. L. REV. 1 (1968); Carl S. Shoup, *Rules for Distributing a Free Government Service Among Areas of a City*, 42 NAT'L TAX J. 103, 110 (1989); Frederick T. Goldberg, Note, *Equalization of Municipal Services: The Economics of* Serrano *and* Shaw, 82 YALE L. J. 89 (1972); Note, *The Right to Adequate Municipal Services: Thoughts and Proposals*, 44 N.Y.U. L. REV. 753 (1969); Clayton P. Gillette, *Equality and Variety in the Delivery of Municipal Services*, 100 HARV. L. REV. 946 (1987) (book review).

24. For discussion of the evidence of discrimination in mortgage lending, *see e.g.*,

Glen B. Canner & Delores S. Smith, *Expanded HMDA Data on Residential Lending: One Year Later*, 78 FED. RESERVE BULL. 801 (1992); Glen B. Canner & Delores S. Smith, *Home Mortgage Disclosure Act: Expanded Data on Residential Lending*, 77 FED. RESERVE BULL. 859 (1991).

25. For a summary of the literature about the downward spiral that may result from declines in neighborhood quality, and increases in the concentration of poverty that may be associated with such declines, see Michael H. Schill, *Deconcentrating the Inner City Poor*, 67 CHI.-KENT L. REV. 795, 804-07 (1991).

26. San Antonio Indep. Sch. Dist. v Rodriguez , 411 U.S. 1 (1973). Under various theories of fairness, e.g., John Rawls' Difference Principle, however, such discrimination against the poor would be unfair and would justify changes in the siting process. JOHN RAWLS, A THEORY OF JUSTICE 75-83 (1971).

27. Village of Arlington Heights v. Metropolitan Hous. Dev. Corp., 429 U.S. 252 (1977).

28. Because discrimination against the poor is not unconstitutional, whereas discrimination against people of color is, a claim of racial discrimination might need to separate out the disparate effect that a siting process has upon people of color because of their race from the effect it has upon the people of color because of their poverty.

29. Evidence that the siting process had a disproportionate effect upon people of color does not prove that siting officials intentionally targeted people of color to host the LULUs. Instead, it may be that siting officials chose sites on the basis of land prices, proximity to sources, or any number of other nondiscriminitory factors, but that the use of those factors unintentionally resulted in a siting pattern that disproportionately affected people of color. Nevertheless, evidence of disproportionate effect, if accompanied by other indicia of racial animus, may be probative of discriminatory intent. *See* Village of Arlington Heights v. Metropolitan Hous. Dev. Corp., 429 U.S. 252, 265-66 (1977); *see also* R.I.S.E. v. Kay, 768 F. Supp. 1144, 1149 (E.D. Va. 1991); East Bibb Twiggs Neighborhood Ass'n v. Macon-Bibb County Planning & Zoning Comm'n, 706 F. Supp. 880, 884 (M.D. Ga. 1989), *aff'd*, 896 F.2d 1264 (11th Cir. 989); Bean v. Southwestern Waste Management Corp., 482 F. Supp. 673, 678 (S.D. Tex. 1979), *aff'd*, 782 F.2d 1038 (5th Cir. 1986). Under some statutory schemes, the disproportionate effect of a siting could be considered a disparate impact and be actionable even without a finding of discriminatory intent. *See, e.g.,* Huntington Branch, NAACP v. Town of Huntington, 844 F.2d 926, 936-37 (2d Cir. 1988), *aff'd*, 488 U.S. 15 (1988) (The Fair Housing Act, 42 U.S.C. §§ 3601-19, requires only a finding of disparate impact); NAACP v. Medical center, Inc., 657 F.2d 1322, 1328-31 (3d Cir. 1981) (Title VI of the Civil Rights Act of 1964, 42 U.S.C. § 2000d, requires only a finding of disparate impact, at least where regulations implementing the statute specify a disparate impact standard). In addition, under some theories of discrimination, at least some forms of disparate impact should be actionable. *See, e.g.,* LAURENCE H. TRIBE, AMERICAN CONSTITUTIONAL LAW §16-21, at 1514-21 (2d ed. 1988); Paul Brest, *The Supreme Court, 1975 Term—Foreword: In Defense of the Antidiscrimination Principle*, 90 HARV. L. REV. 1, 22-53 (1976); Theodore Eisenberg, *Disproportionate Impact and Illicit Motive: Theories of Constitutional Adjudication*, 52 N.Y.U. L. REV. 36,422-83 (1977); Owen M. Fiss, *Groups and the Equal Protection Clause*, 5 PHIL & PUB. AFF. 107, 141-46, 157-60 (1976); Owen M. Fiss, *A Theory of Fair Employment Laws*, 38 U. CHI. L. REV. 235, 244-65 (1971). To avoid the implication that a finding of disproportionate effect necessarily leads to a finding of an illegal disparate impact, I refer to any disparity in the impact of siting decisions as "disproportionate effect."

30. If the market forces at issue are based upon discrimination, i.e., if host neighborhoods became predominantly minority after the LULU was sited because racial discrimination in the housing market relegated people of color to those neighborhoods, siting practices might have to change to account for persistent discrimination in the housing market. *Cf.* United States v. Yonkers Bd. of Educ., 624 F. Supp. 1276, 1531-37 (S.D.N.Y. 1985) (noting that existence of housing discrimination may be relevant to determination of liability for segregation of schools).

31. For discussion of whether proposals to make the siting process fairer might be appropriate even if market dynamics might soon undermine the fairness of the distribution, *see* Been, *supra* note 3, at 1018-24.

32. The studies discussed in this Article focus on the location of LULUs. Other studies show that the poor and people of color bear a disproportionate share of the general burdens of pollution and of the costs of cleaning up pollution, but do not specifically address the burden of hosting polluting LULUs. For reviews of that literature, see Cole,

*supra* note 1, at 622-27 & nn.8-18; Maureen L. Cropper & Wallace E. Oates, *Environmental Economics: A Survey*, 30 J. ECON. LITERATURE 675, 727-28 (1992). Lazarus, *supra* note 4, at 796-801; Paul Mohai & Bunyan Bryant, *Environmental Injustice: Weighing Race and Class as Factors in the Distribution of Environmental Hazards*, 63 U. COLO. L. REV. 921, 925-27 (1992). Studies also show that environmental laws are enforced less vigorously in poor and minority communities. *See* Lavelle & Coyle, *supra* note 22; Zimmerman, *supra* note 22; *see also* Lazarus, *supra* note 4, at 818-19 & nn.125-33 (surveying the literature); *Cf.* CLEAN SITES, HAZARDOUS WASTE SITES AND THE RURAL POOR: A PRELIMINARY ASSESSMENT 50-51 (1990) (finding that hazardous waste sites in rural poor counties were more likely to have been cleaned up than in other counties, without addressing the racial characteristics of the counties). *But see* Hird, *supra* note 22, at 337 (finding no relationship between the pace at which sites are cleaned up and the host county's socioeconomic characteristics).

33. CRJ REPORT, *supra* note 2.

34. The 415 facilities comprised all of the facilities in the contiguous United States that could be identified through the Environmental Protection Agency's Hazardous Waste Data Management System (HWDMS). *Id.* at 10, 65. The HWDMS was an early version of the Resource Conservation and Recovery Information System.

35. The study also examined the demographics of communities that contained uncontrolled hazardous waste sites that the Environmental Protection Agency has identified as posing a potential threat to the environment and to public health and has listed in the Comprehensive Environmental Response, Compensation, and Liability System (CERCLIS). CRJ REPORT, *supra* note 2, at 3-4, 53. The study found that 57% of all African-Americans and Latinos live in communities hosting such facilities, while 54% of all whites live in such communities. *Id.* at 53; *see also* Zimmerman, *supra* note 22, at 657 (finding that African-Americans are about 50% more likely to live in a community with a CERCLIS site deemed sufficiently hazardous to be placed on the National Priorities List).

36. Commercial hazardous waste facilities are public or private facilities that accept hazardous waste from third parties for a fee for the purpose of treating, storing or disposing of the waste. CRJ REPORT, *supra* note 2, at 65.

37. The CRJ REPORT considered a correlation to be significant at the 90% confidence level. Accordingly, there is a 1 in 10 probability that some of the findings of the study were chance occurrences. *Id.* at 11. For criticisms of the methodology of the CRJ, see Lazarus, *supra* note 4, at 802 n.56.

38. CRJ REPORT, *supra* note 2, at 13, 41-44.

39. *Id.*

40. In addition to the studies discussed in the text, see LAURETTA M. BURKE, ENVIRONMENTAL EQUITY IN LOS ANGELES (National Center for Geographic Information and Analysis Technical Report 93-6,1993) (in Los Angeles, the poorer the area and the higher the percentage of minorities in the population, the greater the number of polluting facilities in the area); CITIZENS FOR A BETTER ENVIRONMENT, RICHMOND AT RISK: COMMUNITY DEMOGRAPHICS AND TOXIC HAZARDS FROM INDUSTRIAL POLLUTERS 2 121-22 (1989)(residents of Richmond, California census tracts closest to polluting industrial facilities are disproportionately people of color and the poor); PAT COSTNER & JOE THORNTON, PLAYING WITH FIRE: HAZARDOUS WASTE INCINERATION 48-49 (1990)(minority percentage of population in communities hosting or proposed to host hazardous waste incinerators was 89% and 60% higher, respectively, than the national average); BENJAMIN A. GOLDMAN, THE TRUTH ABOUT WHERE YOU LIVE 282-83 (1991) (in those counties that rank the worst on various measures of the presence of toxic substances, the percentage of the population that is minority is more than twice that of the average for other counties); JAY M. GOULD, QUALITY OF LIFE IN AMERICAN NEIGHBORHOODS: LEVELS OF AFFLUENCE, TOXIC WASTE, AND CANCER MORTALITY IN RESIDENTIAL ZIP CODE AREAS 21-24 (1986)(finding that communities with the highest incomes have the lowest amount of toxic waste generated); MICHAEL R. GREENBERG & RICHARD F. ANDERSON, HAZARDOUS WASTE SITES: THE CREDIBILITY GAP (1984) (study of New Jersey's 567 communities indicated that communities with the greatest number of hazardous waste sites tend to have more poor, elderly, young, and African-American residents than other communities); E.B. Attah, *Demographics and Siting Issues in EPA Region IV, in* PROCEEDINGS OF THE CLARK ATLANTA UNIVERSITY AND ENVIRONMENTAL PROTECTION AGENCY REGION IB CONFERENCE ON ENVIRONMENTAL EQUITY 3-4 (Bob Holmes ed., 1992) (study of CERCLIS sites in 8 southeastern states revealed that number of sites per census tract increases as the percentage of the tract's population that is minority increases);

Greenberg, *supra* note 2, at 241-43, 244-46 (finding that large waste-to-energy facilities (WTEFs) in towns of at least 100,000 residents were located in towns that were poorer and had more minorities as a percentage of the population than the "service area" of the facility, and that when population data was weighted to take into account the fact that people of color tend to be located in cities , the percentage of the population comprised of African-Americans was 65% higher in cities that hosted WTEFs than in the United States as a whole); Kusum Ketkar, *Hazardous Waste Sites and Property Values in the State of New Jersey*, 24 APPLIED ECON. 647, 653 (1992) (analysis of 62 municipalities in seven urban counties in New Jersey "implies that the municipalities that have high property tax rates and a greater proportion of minorities also have a larger number of [hazardous waste] sites," without separating the effect of race from the effect of high property tax rates); Mohai & Bryant, *supra* note 32, at 5 (finding that people of color in Detroit were almost four times more likely than whites to live within one mile of a waste facility); Harvey L. White, *Hazardous Waste Incineration and Minority Communities*, in RACE AND THE INCIDENCE OF ENVIRONMENTAL HAZARDS: A TIME FOR DISCOURSE 126, 132 (Bunyan Bryant & Paul Mohai eds., 1992) [hereinafter INCIDENCE] (in Baton Rouge area, minority communities had average of one hazardous waste incineration facility per 7349 residents, while white communities had only one site per 31,100 residents); Jane Kay, *Minorities Bear Brunt of Pollution*, S.F. EXAMINER, Apr. 7, 1991, at A1, A12 (Los Angeles County zip code area with largest amount of waste discharge is predominantly African-American and Latino); Dennis Pfaff, *Pollution and the Poor*, DETROIT NEWS, Nov. 26, 1989, at A1 (41 of Detroit's top air polluters, 25 of the 33 sites most contaminated with toxic chemicals, and four of five licensed hazardous waste treatment and storage facilities are located in neighborhoods with average per capita incomes of less than $10,000 per year); Kevin L. Brown, Environmental Discrimination: Myth or Reality 17-18 (Mar. 29, 1991) (unpublished manuscript, on file with author)(random sample of predominantly minority census tracts in St. Louis had 47% more chemical emissions than comparable sample of predominantly white census tracts). For comprehensive discussions of the existing research, see Been, *supra* note 3, at 1009-15; Cole, *supra* note 1, at 622-23 nn.8-9, 625 n.17; Lazarus, *supra* note 4, at 801-06.

41. GAO REPORT, *supra* note 4.

42. GAO REPORT, *supra* note 4, at 4. The landfill in Warren County, North Carolina is sited in an area that was 66% African-American and is within four miles of an area that was 47% American Indian. *Id*. at app. I, 7.

43. *Id*. at app. I, 1, 5, 7.

44. *Id*. at 4.

45. *Id*. at app. I, 1, 5, 7.

46. Bullard, *Solid Waste*, *supra* note 9.

47. ROBERT D. BULLARD, INVISIBLE HOUSTON 60-75 (1987).

48. BULLARD, *supra* note 1.

49. Bullard, *Solid Waste*, *supra* note 9, at 279-83. Tables 1 and 2 of *Solid Waste* List five incinerators and three mini-incinerators, and describe four of the incinerators and two of the mini-incinerators as located in African-American neighborhoods. Tables 3,5, and 6 list five "City of Houston Municipal Landfill Sites," six "Texas Department of Health Permitted Municipal Landfills Sites," and six "Browning Ferris Industries Landfill Sites," for a total of 17 landfills. Of those, all but two are described as located in African-American neighborhoods. Although Professor Bullard does not total the numbers from the different tables, the "bottom line" to be drawn from his study is that six of the eight incinerators and mini-incinerators, and 15 of the 17 landfills, or 21 of 25 sites, are in African-American neighborhoods. Of the four sites that were in non-African-American neighborhoods, Bullard's study showed that two were located in a neighborhood that was undergoing transition from a white to an African-American community (the two landfills actually are the same site, *see infra* text accompanying note 70), and one was located in a Hispanic neighborhood. Only one of the sites was adjacent to a predominantly white community. Bullard, *Solid Waste*, *supra* note 9, at 279-83.

50. In correspondence with the author, Professor Bullard states that his study was based on host neighborhood demographics as of the census closest to the year that the site was opened. Letter from Robert D. Bullard to Vicki Been (Mar. 18, 1993)(on file with author). None of his published accounts of the study specify the date of the data use. In the first published account, Professor Bullard's list of references includes a citation only to 1980 Census Bureau data. Bullard, *Solid Waste*, *supra* note 9, at 288. Neither of the later books drawing on that study includes any citation to specific census data. Pro-

fessor Bullard originally prepared his research to present in Bean v. Southwestern Waste Management Corp., 482 F. Supp. 673 (S.D. Tex. 1979), *aff'd*, 782 F.2d 1039 (5th Cir. 1986). Professor Bullard's testimony in that litigation refers to an exhibit in which he presented data about the racial composition of host census tracts in 1970, 1975, and 1979. Transcript of Proceedings, Nov. 27, 1979, at 345, Bean v. Southwestern Waste Management Corp., 482 F. Supp. 673 (S.D. Tex 1979) (Civ. No. H-79-2215), *aff'd*, 782 F.2d 1039 (5th Cir. 1986) [hereinafter Bean Transcript]. At other points in the testimony, Professor Bullard presents analyses that were based solely on 1979 data. *Id.* at 351. Efforts to verify which of the various analyses that Professor Bullard presented in the litigation formed the basis for the conclusions reported in *Solid Waste* have been unsuccessful. Professor Bullard responded to the author's request for his original data by referring her to the litigation files. The clerk of the court in which the litigation was filed has destroyed the court's copy of all exhibits, however, and the defendants and their lawyers no longer have copies in their files. Telephone Interview with Boone Vastine, Attorney with Browning Ferris Industries (Sept. 2, 1993). In any event, Professor Bullard's *Solid Waste* study does not remedy the gaps in the evidence identified earlier in the Article, *see supra* text accompanying notes 3-7, because it does not focus on the question of how the waste facilities affected the demographics of the surrounding neighborhoods.

51. Although both the CRJ and the GAO studies admit that they do not show cause and effect, CRJ REPORT, *supra* note 2, at 11, GAO REPORT, *supra* note 4, at 3, many discussions of the evidence make causal assertions. Indeed, some environmental justice advocates claim that the evidence supports the charge that siting choices are intentionally discriminatory. Grossman, *supra* note 1, at 31 (quoting Rev. Benjamin Chavis, then Executive Director of Commission for Racial Justice, and one of founders of environmental justice movement, as alleging that developers and siting officials "deliberate[ly] target[ ] . . . people of color communities for toxic waste facilities"); *see also Have Minorities Benefited . . . ? A Forum*, 18 EPA J., Mar.-Apr. 1992, at 32, 36 (comments of Beverly Wright) ("[F]ederal, state, and local agencies and industries . . . target [low income] communities for the siting of undesirable 'but necessary' polluting facilities.").

52. Hamilton, *supra* note 4, at 106-20.

53. Expansion decisions are much less controversial than initial siting decisions, but nevertheless generate opposition. The decision to expand capacity involves some of the same factors as the initial siting decision, such as the site's proximity to potential customers. Accordingly, to the extent that any disproportionate effect arising from siting decisions can be traced to siters' propensity to take the "path of least resistance," or to consider such factors as proximity to potential customers, expansion decisions should also have a disproportionate effect.

54. Hamilton, *supra* note 4, at 116-18.

55. *Id.* at 120.

56. *Id.* at 120-22.

57. *Id.* at 121.

58. Other studies have used county-level data as well. *See, e.g.*, Hird, *supra* note 22. For a full discussion of the appropriate level of data aggregation, see *infra* text accompanying notes 73-84.

59. For a discussion of the problem of correlating siting dates and the decennial censuses, see *infra* note 62.

60. The GAO gives the dates repeated in the text as the dates on which the landfills were "established." The GAO never defined what it meant by "established," but conversations with regulators indicate that the sites began to operate as offsite disposal facilities in those years. Telephone Interview with Willie Morgan, Environmental Engineer, Hazardous Waste Section, South Carolina Department of Health and Environmental Control (June 26, 1992); Telephone Interview with Allan Tinsley, Section Manager, Compliance and Monitoring, Division of Compliance, Monitoring, and Enforcement, South Carolina Department of Health and Environmental Control (June 30, 1992); Telephone Interview with Gary Alberg, Permitting Engineer, Solid Waste Division, North Carolina Department of Environment Health and Natural Resources (June 17, 1992); Telephone Interview with Tracey Williams, Environmental Engineer, Alabama Department of Environmental Protection (June 29 & 30, 1992).

61. *See, e.g.*, Charles J. McDermott, *Environmental Equity: A Waste Manager's Perspective*, LAND USE F., Winter 1993, at 12, 14-15 (describing siting process for Chemical Waste facility in Sumter County, Alabama as beginning in 1974).

62. It would be preferable, of course, to use data from 1975 for the facilities opening in 1977. Data are unavailable for intervals between the 1970 and 1980 censuses, however, so the correlation between the siting date and the census data is less than ideal. The 1970 data are more appropriate than 1980 data for the analysis of sites opened in 1977, however, because the siting decisionmakers were likely to have had only the 1970 data at the time they made their siting decisions.

63. For criticism of the measure of disproportion implicit in the GAO and Bullard studies (and followed by the extensions of those studies reported here), see *supra* note 2.

64. Several explanations might be offered for the decrease in the percentage of the host communities' African-American population. The waste facilities may have brought jobs to the communities. Attracted by those jobs, whites may have immigrated to the area, displacing African-Americans. Alternatively, the waste facilities, or land uses they spawned (such as housing for their workers) may have displaced African-American housing and thereby driven African-Americans from the neighborhood. *See* Dubin, *supra* note 5, at 794-97 (discussing various forms of discriminatory zoning); Rabin, *supra* note 5, at 107-18 (examples of expulsive zoning). To assess which of these (or other) factors might account for the changes in the communities' demographics would require a case study that is beyond the scope of this [viewpoint].

65. The GAO study reported the poverty rate of each host community. Those figures do not prove that a community's poverty made it more likely to be chosen as host to the facility, because they do not indicate the community's standing among other communities "competing" for the LULU. Only by analyzing the community's poverty relative to that of the entire state, "service region" of the facility, or nation can one ascertain whether a community's poverty made it more likely to be chosen to host a facility. . . .

66. The largest change was a 15% increase in the relative median family income of Sumter County between 1970 and 1990.

67. It might be preferable to compare the host county subdivision (rather than the host county) to the host state, *see infra* text accompanying notes 73-84, but published data about poverty and median house value are unavailable for the county subdivisions in 1970, and data about median family income for county subdivisions are unavailable for both 1970 and 1980. . . . Changes in the relative poverty and relative median house value between 1980 and 1990 were generally more pronounced in the county subdivisions than in the host counties. Those data do not reveal any clear trend, however: two of the county subdivisions became significantly less poor relative to the host states between 1980 and 1990, while one became significantly more poor and one remained the same. Similarly, in two of the county subdivisions, relative median housing value increased between 1980 and 1990, but in the other two, it decreased.

68. Bullard, *Solid Waste, supra* note 9, at 279-83; *see also supra* note 49. Professor Bullard's descriptions of the racial composition of the host communities do not correspond to census tract data for either 1980 or the census closest to the date the site was permitted. *See infra* text accompanying note 72.

69. Professor Bullard does not explain whether the six "Texas Department of Health Permitted Municipal Landfill Sites" and six "Browning Ferris Industries Landfill Sites" he studied cover the entire universe of sites that fall into those categories. If Professor Bullard analyzed fewer than all of the sites in those categories, his conclusions about the disproportionate siting of facilities obviously would be inaccurate. In explaining the study that served as the basis for Bullard, *Solid Waste, supra* note 9, during the course of the litigation for which the study was prepared, Professor Bullard stated that there were 76 solid waste sites in the study. Bean Transcript, *supra* note 50, at 374, 398-99. Earlier, he had submitted an exhibit analyzing 34 sites. *Id* at 399. In its decision, the *Bean* court states that 17 sites were operating with Texas Department of Health (TDH) permits as of July 1, 1978. Bean v. Southwestern Waste Management Corp., 482 F. Supp. 673, 677 (S.D. Tex. 1979) *aff'd*, 782 F.2d 1038 (5th Cir. 1986). The six sites identified as TDH sites in *Solid Waste* accordingly appear to be only a subset of sites that should have been included.

70. The three landfills that fall into both categories are the American Refuse Systems facility at 1140 Holmes Road, the Browning Ferris Industries facility at the same address, *see infra* note 71, and the Browning Ferris Industries facility at 11013 Beaumont Highway.

71. Professor Bullard counts the sites as separate landfills because the Texas Department of Health issued two permits for the landfill. Letter from Robert D. Bullard to Vicki Been (Mar. 18, 1993) (on file with author).

72. *Id.* Professor Bullard's testimony in the litigation for which he prepared the study helps to illustrate his approach to defining a "neighborhood." There, in explaining why he considered the two Ruffino sites to be located in an African-American community, he testified that although the data for the census tract in which the sites were located indicated that the tract was predominantly white, his "ethnographic" study and "field observations" of the areas showed that there was a "cluster" of African-Americans close to the site. Bean Transcript, *supra* note 50, at 382-87, 403.

73. For discussion of the problem of selecting the appropriate level of analysis for environmental justice studies, *see* Been, *supra* note 3, at 1014-15; Greenberg, *supra* note 2, at 238; Rae Zimmerman, *Issues of Classification in Environmental Equity: How We Manage Is How We Measure*, FORDHAM URB. L. J. (forthcoming 1994) (manuscript at 13-28, on file with author) (discussing various definitions of neighborhood that can be used in environmental equity studies and problems raised in selection of definition); *see also* CRJ REPORT, *supra* note 2, at 61-62 (advocating five-digit zip code areas as best unit of analysis); Zimmerman, *supra* note 22, at 7-9 (advocating municipality as unit of analysis); East Bibb Twiggs Neighborhood Ass'n v. Macon-Bibb County Planning & Zoning Comm'n, 706 F. Supp. 880, 884 (M.D. Ga. 1989), *aff'd*, 896 F.2d 1264 (11th Cir. 1989) (census tract is appropriate unit of analysis). Whatever level of analysis is eventually chosen as the most appropriate for environmental justice studies, researchers will face the additional question of how to address sites that do not fall in the center of the tract or other unit of analysis, but are instead at the border of two or more units. In the extensions reported here, when a site was at the border of a tract, the host tract and the bordering tract were combined for the analysis.

74. *See generally* Allan C. Goodman, *A Comparison of Block Group and Census Tract Data in a Hedonic Housing Price Model*, 53 LAND ECON. 483 (1977) (advocating use of "block groups" for measuring neighborhood values).

75. Studies of the property value impacts of waste facilities, for example, show effects on homes miles away from the site. *See, e.g.*, GERALD E. SMOLEN ET AL., ECONOMIC EFFECTS OF HAZARDOUS WASTE LANDFILLS ON SURROUNDING REAL ESTATE VALUES IN TOLEDO, OHIO 22 (Ohio State Univ., Center for Real Estate Educ. and Research, Research Report No. 44, Feb. 1991) (finding that announcement of proposed low-level nuclear waste site adversely affected prices of property as far as 5.75 miles away); Janet E. Kohlhase, *The Impact of Toxic Waste Sites on Housing Values*, 30 J. URB. ECON. 1, 14-15 (1991) (finding negative effects up to 6.2 miles from toxic waste sites following announcement of area as Superfund priority site); *Cf.* Hays B. Gamble & Roger H. Downing, *Effects of Sanitary Landfills on Property Values and Residential Development, in* SOLID AND LIQUID WASTES: MANAGEMENT, METHODS AND SOCIOECONOMIC CONSIDERATIONS 350, 358 (S.K. Majumdar & E. Willard Miller eds., 1984) (finding that sanitary landfills adversely affect prices of properties on the main access roads to landfill within one mile of the landfill, but did not affect developed residential properties near landfills). Because the studies of property value impacts do not clearly establish the boundaries of the area affected by a LULU, it may be that census tracts also are generally too small to capture the impact of the LULU. The studies make quite clear, however, that the impact of a LULU is felt beyond the block on which it is located. Census blocks accordingly are less likely to be the appropriate unit of analysis than census tracts.

76. MICHAEL J. WHITE, AMERICAN NEIGHBORHOODS AND RESIDENTIAL DIFFERENTIATION 290 (1987).

77. *Id.*

78. *Id.* at 290; BUREAU OF THE CENSUS, U.S. DEP'T OF COMMERCE, 1990 CPH 3-42, 1990 CENSUS OF POPULATION AND HOUSING, POPULATION AND HOUSING CHARACTERISTICS FOR CENSUS TRACTS AND BLOCK NUMBERING AREAS, SOUTH CAROLINA (OUTSIDE METROPOLITAN AREAS) A-4 (1993). Many areas of the United States were not block numbered until the 1990 census, so comparison of block statistics across decades is impossible. BUREAU OF THE CENSUS, U.S. DEP'T OF COMMERCE, 1990 CPH 3-42, 1990 CENSUS OF POPULATION AND HOUSING, POPULATION AND HOUSING CHARACTERISTICS FOR CENSUS TRACTS AND BLOCK NUMBERING AREAS, SOUTH CAROLINA A-3 (1993). While there was an equivalent to block groups, called "enumeration districts," used prior to the 1990 census, differences between the enumeration districts and block groups make comparisons across decades difficult.

79. WHITE, *supra* note 76, at 290.

80. *Id.* When a tract grows beyond the standard size, it typically is split into subtracts. In the extension reported here, when a tract was split into sub-tracts, the subtracts were re-combined to make the comparison across decades as accurate as possible.

81. *Id.*

82. *Id.* at 293.

83. *See id.* at 297.

84. Mohai & Bryant draw circles at one and one-and-one-half mile radii from sites for their analysis, rather than using standard census units. Paul Mohai & Bunyan Bryant, *Environmental Racism: Reviewing the Evidence, in* INCIDENCE, *supra* note 40, at 163, 170-76. The CRJ REPORT, *supra* note 2, at 9, uses five-digit zip-code areas, which may be smaller or larger than census tracts, but typically are larger than census blocks or block groupings.

85. This conclusion assumes that the facilities Professor Bullard studied were a complete set of the TDH and Browning Ferris landfills in existence at the time of his study. That assumption may not be correct. *See supra* text accompanying note 69. The conclusion also assumes that proportionality should be measured by comparing the percentage of African-Americans in the host tracts to the percentage in non-host tracts. See *supra* note 2 for criticisms of that measure of proportionality.

86. A poverty rate is considered significantly higher for the purposes of this study if it is more than 110% of the rate for Harris County. An alternative method would measure the number of LULUs sited in neighborhoods whose poverty rates were within one or two standard deviations of the Houston rate. Yet another method would examine the percentage of LULUs sited in neighborhoods that fall into the bottom quartile or quintile of all Houston neighborhoods, sorted by poverty rates, median income, or mean income.

87. In the neighborhoods surrounding the mini-incinerators, relative housing values declined in one neighborhood following the siting, but increased in the other two neighborhoods. The data on mini-incinerators is of limited use, however, because all the mini-incinerators had ceased to operate by the mid 1970's and to the extent that they were not expected to re-open, any effect they may have had on property values could easily have been erased by 1980.

88. Median rents remained fairly stable in all but two of the neighborhoods. In one of the exceptional neighborhoods, relative rents fell significantly, while in the other, relative rents increased significantly. In theory, rents surrounding an undesirable land use should fall. If there is a shortage of housing that is affordable and accessible to African-Americans and the poor, however, demand might keep the rental prices stable even though the LULU has made the neighborhood less desirable.

89. Again, this conclusion assumes that Professor Bullard included in his study all of the TDH and Browning Ferris landfills in existence at the time of his study. *See supra* note 69.

90. In the Houston subdivision of Harris County, only 45% of the population lived in the same residence in 1985 and 1990. BUREAU OF THE CENSUS, U.S. DEP'T OF COMMERCE, 1990 CPH 3-176C, 1990 CENSUS OF POPULATION AND HOUSING, POPULATION AND HOUSING CHARACTERISTICS FOR CENSUS TRACTS AND BLOCK NUMBERING AREAS, HOUSTON-GALVESTON-BRAZORIA, TX CMSA, HOUSTON, TX PMSA SECTION 2 OF 3, 843 (1993). In the areas covered by the GAO study, in contrast, the percentage of the population living in the same residence in which they had lived five years earlier was 64% in Sumter County, Alabama; 69% in Chester County, South Carolina; 50% in Sumter County, South Carolina; and 68% in Warren County, North Carolina. BUREAU OF THE CENSUS, U.S. DEP'T OF COMMERCE, 1990 CPH 3-2, 1990 CENSUS OF POPULATION AND HOUSING, POPULATION AND HOUSING CHARACTERISTICS FOR CENSUS TRACTS AND BLOCK NUMBERING AREAS, ALABAMA 360 (1993); BUREAU OF THE CENSUS, U.S. DEP'T OF COMMERCE, 1990 CPH 3-35, 1990 CENSUS OF POPULATION AND HOUSING, POPULATION AND HOUSING CHARACTERISTICS FOR CENSUS TRACTS AND BLOCK NUMBERING AREAS, NORTH CAROLINA 610 (1993); BUREAU OF THE CENSUS, U.S. DEP'T OF COMMERCE, 1990 CPH 3-42, 1990 CENSUS OF POPULATION AND HOUSING, POPULATION AND HOUSING CHARACTERISTICS FOR CENSUS TRACTS AND BLOCK NUMBERING AREAS, SOUTH CAROLINA 310 (1993).

91. The Chemical Waste facility in Sumter County, Alabama, for example, employs 300 people, 60% of whom live in Sumter County. McDermott, *supra* note 61, at 15; *see also supra* note 64.

# 4

# Native Americans
# Must Fight to Prevent
# Environmental Injustice
# on Their Homelands

## Gail Small

*Gail Small, a Rockefeller Fellow at the University of Colorado, is executive director of Native Action, a nonprofit activist organization based in Lame Deer, Montana, where the author has been working since the 1970s to protect the environment of the Northern Cheyenne Reservation.*

The Northern Cheyenne Reservation in southeastern Montana is surrounded by coal companies who want to stripmine the reservation land. In the 1970s the Bureau of Indian Affairs (BIA), the government agency charged with promoting the welfare of Native Americans, leased over half the reservation to these companies. For the next fifteen years the Cheyenne, who were poor to begin with, spent most of their resources trying to reverse the BIA's action. The case of the Cheyenne is just one example of the environmental battles confronting Indian tribes nationwide as government and industry seek out reservation lands for their resources and for their use as dumping grounds for nuclear and other hazardous waste. For the Cheyenne and other Native Americans, more than a few rivers and trees are at stake—the environment is integral to tribal religion and is inseparable from the Native American way of life.

M y tribe, the Northern Cheyenne, lives on 500,000 acres of beautiful ponderosa pine country in southeastern Montana. Our reservation has tremendous cultural significance for us. Two years after the Cheyenne defeated Custer at the Battle of Little Bighorn, they were taken as prisoners of war in reprisal, and marched to Indian Territory in what is now Oklahoma. Tribal oral tradition states that the Cheyenne were quickly dying there of malaria and other diseases, and agreed that they would rather die fighting to return to their beloved northland than die of the white man's diseases, as his prisoners.

The Cheyenne told the U.S. government agent that they were leaving for their homeland, and asked him to let them get a short distance from the fort before bloodying the ground. Only a few hundred Cheyenne survived this walk north. Our reservation thus represents the blood and tears of our grandparents, who willingly gave their lives so that we might live here.

## Surrounded

The Cheyenne now find our reservation being surrounded by the largest coal stripmines in this country, and the threat that the mines will encroach on our own land is ever-present. I have been involved in the fight to protect our reservation and southeastern Montana from coal mining since the 1970s, when I was in high school. It was then that the Cheyenne learned the horrifying news that the Bureau of Indian Affairs had leased over half our reservation for stripmining, at the paltry rate of 17 cents per ton, with no environmental safeguards included in the leases.

Every resource of our small tribe was committed to the battle against those leases. The enormity of our situation frightened and angered us. I was one of several young Cheyenne sent by the tribe to investigate coal mines in Navaho country and Wyoming; at one point, twenty of us had our picture taken standing inside a huge coal shovel, to demonstrate the size of the industrial operation that coal mining would bring to our land. After college, I served on the tribal committee charged with voiding the leases—the only member with a college degree. We were fortunate to find a capable young attorney with a passion for Indians and for justice, but it took almost fifteen years of anxiety and sacrifices by the people before the Northern Cheyenne convinced Congress to void the coal leases.

Today, however, Cheyenne coal has become still more valuable. There are no coal mines on my reservation yet, and no coal leases have been signed. But every year, the tribe debates again whether we can afford to continue refusing the offers of the coal companies. And every year the mines on nearby land come closer. Current plans call for opening up the Powder River Country (our best hunting grounds) by building a railroad directly along the Tongue River (our major water source). Our most traditional village, the Birney community, is directly across the river from the site of the proposed railroad and the five new coal mines.

---

*Our reservation . . . represents the blood and tears of our grandparents, who willingly gave their lives so that we might live here.*

---

The Northern Cheyenne are not the only Indians who face such problems. Tribes across the country find their lands aggressively sought after for their energy resources and as dumping grounds for America's waste. Indian tribes own over a third of the low-sulfur coal west of the Mississippi, as much as half of the privately owned uranium in the country, and sizable reserves of oil, natural gas, and oil shale. The instability and depletion of world energy supplies—along with the 1990 Clean Air Act Amendments, which favor low-sulfur coal—have increased the pressure for these reserves. Promises of overnight wealth to impoverished tribes serve to divide and conquer the people, as federal agencies, energy corporations, and private speculators seek to dump nuclear waste or get rich off Indian land.

By necessity, then, Indian tribes are major players in the environmental justice movement. Their legal situation, however, is unique. It derives from their status as the indigenous peoples and the original landlords of this country.

Indian reservations represent an American legal quid pro quo: in return for relinquishing claim to thousands of acres of their aboriginal lands, the tribes reserved for themselves homelands and various other rights in the treaties they negotiated with the United States. The premise of the Reserved Rights Doctrine is that the treaties were not a grant of rights to the Indians, but rather a reservation of rights they already possessed. Many past judicial decisions have complicated what is now known as tribal sovereignty, but the tribal right of self-government has been repeatedly affirmed by the U.S. Supreme Court, and the tribes' jurisdiction over their homelands remains substantially intact.

## Government as "trustee"

Another factor complicating tribal sovereignty is the unique trust relationship between the federal government, specifically Congress, and the Indian tribes. The federal government, as trustee, asserts plenary power over Indian tribes (under the legal rhetoric that we need protecting). In general, federal laws apply on reservations, although tribal governments have the inherent right to establish tribal environmental laws that are stronger than the federal statutes. Because the trust relationship preempts jurisdiction by the states, it has served to safeguard Indian rights and resources and preserve Indian self-government. The trust relationship also requires that any action by the federal government, or its agencies, affecting Indian property or rights be consistent with the most exacting fiduciary standards.

As self-governing entities, tribes have the legal authority for environmental regulation and enforcement of tribal environmental laws; they also have the proprietary and police powers for environmental protection. Why, then, is it so difficult for Indian tribes to protect their environments? One reason is that, as the Northern Cheyenne found when we fought the coal leases in court during the 1970s and 1980s, it is extremely difficult for Indian tribes to sue our federal trustee for breach of trust.

Another reason, which cannot be underestimated, is that no significant federal assistance has ever been provided to develop the tribal government infrastructure necessary for environmental protection. In fact, fiduciary standards or no, only a dime of every dollar appropriated by Congress for Indians ever reaches the reservations. Most of the monies are eaten by the massive bureaucracy of the Bureau of Indian Affairs. (And yet, when it is a question of the study and development of coal mines, uranium mines, and nuclear waste dumps on reservations, federal funds always appear.)

My tribe experienced this problem in 1977, when, seeing the coal mines growing larger and coming closer, our tribal leaders decided to protect our air quality. They petitioned the U.S. Environmental Protection Agency (EPA) for the right to designate our air quality as Class I, among the cleanest in the country, and to apply the most stringent air-quality standards. The Northern Cheyenne tribe was the first government entity to take this step—but we had to lead the EPA by the hand for more than ten years before it acknowledged that we were a government, with the right to funding and enforcement authority under the 1990 Clean Air Act. Almost twenty years later, the Northern Cheyenne are still fighting this battle. We were eventually forced to settle with the coal companies in a lawsuit we had brought over some nearby power plants, simply to get the funds to establish air quality monitoring stations on the reservation.

## Desperate needs

As tribes begin to draft and enact their own environmental laws, the need for government infrastructure is becoming more desperate. Tribal environmental protection agencies must be adequately funded and staffed to implement these laws, tribal courts to enforce them. And the monies should go directly to the tribes, not to the various intermediary organizations that claim to provide technical assistance.

This means that it is not enough for our federal trustee simply to amend environmental laws by acknowledging tribal governments for "substantially the same treatment as a state," a step that is now becoming more common. Without adequate funding, the laws will remain law on paper only. At a series of Tribal Issues Workgroups held by EPA's Office of Environmental Equity throughout 1993, tribal delegates informed EPA that it has never fully implemented either the spirit or the letter of the law. Indeed, some tribes declared the phrase "treatment as a state" offensive, considering the longstanding funding inequities.

The funding question is made still more urgent by the general poverty of the tribes. The Northern Cheyenne have refused extravagant offers from the coal companies, while directing every resource we have to the legal battles against coal mining on nearby land. The people have foregone indoor plumbing, roads, and schools for the environmental integrity of this region. It is no small sacrifice. The elderly man who lives next door to my office must use an outhouse, and as I write it is 20 degrees below zero. And our tribe is now fighting the coal boom towns in order to secure a high school of our own for our 400 high-school-aged students, but the boom towns have far more money.

Many younger Cheyenne regard EPA's failure to fund tribal environmental protection as institutional racism. We have also seen this attitude in the white environmental organizations, which failed to respond to our calls for help in fighting mining in the region—even though the mines are destroying pristine wilderness on federal lands. It was my idea to make these requests, and when they went unanswered, our Tribal President told me that I was young and naïve, and that I had to learn to strategize under the assumption that we have few allies. And indeed, it has been my experience that Americans would rather fight for the rainforest than join the battle being waged in their own backyards.

## Saving natural religion

Perhaps this is true partly because opposing world views separate our understanding of the environment from that of other Americans. Indians believe in the spiritual nature of the environment, something that cannot be quantified and cannot be preserved through "mitigation" of environmentally harmful development. As an elder of my tribe has said,

"There is no word in our language for mitigation. We cannot even understand the concept."

The federal agencies charged with helping us protect our environment cannot do so unless they understand this interdependence of environment, culture, and religion in the tribal way of life. When I worked as a tribal sociologist some years ago, I once took a draft tribal water code to the five villages of my reservation for public input. I found that protection of the water spirits was a preeminent concern throughout the reservation, and that the spirits varied depending on whether the water source was a river, lake, or spring. I reported back to the attorneys who had been contracted by the U.S. government to draw up the code, and they laughed at my findings.

> *Every year, the tribe debates again whether we can afford to continue refusing the offers of the coal companies.*

But it was no laughing matter a few years later, when an elderly Cheyenne man with a rifle held off an ARCO drilling team that had planned to lay lines of dynamite across his spring—an archaic practice no longer used in most drilling operations outside Indian reservations. "Today is a good day to die," he said, holding his old hunting rifle before him. I represented him in tribal court the next morning, seeking a restraining order against ARCO. And I cried with him as he told me how the water spirits sometimes came out and danced at this spring.

Eventually, we saved the spring. But whenever the destructive forces threatening Indian reservations prevail, the real loser is the American public; for what is at stake is the last remaining indigenous knowledge of the spiritual and curative powers of this country's environment. And as I write, the coal fight is beginning again on my reservation, as it has every year for the past three decades. Another coal contract is before the Council, the coal company is promising to make every Cheyenne a millionaire, and some are arguing that we must cut off the toe to save the body—that we should lease a small part of the reservation, because we need the white man's money in order to give our children a way out of poverty.

Like many Cheyenne, I feel as if I have already lived a lifetime fighting stripmining. We live with fear, anger, and urgency. And we long for a better life for our tribe.

# 5

# Native Americans Have the Right to Make Their Own Land-Use Decisions

## Skull Valley Goshute Tribe Executive Office

*The Skull Valley Goshutes are a small tribe of approximately 112 members who occupy an 18,000-acre reservation in Tooele County, Utah.*

Until the recent cutbacks in defense spending, the members of the Skull Valley Goshute Tribe derived most of their employment from defense industries. In the face of current and projected cutbacks, the Tribe examined many other employment options. One that has so far found favor with the Tribe is the Monitored Retrieval Storage (M.R.S.) program of the U.S. Department of Energy (DOE), designed to provide temporary storage facilities (for up to 40 years) for spent nuclear fuel rods. The Tribe has embarked on a series of studies of the M.R.S. program, learning that despite media hysteria about "nuclear waste," the storage of nuclear fuel rods is a relatively safe and potentially very lucrative industrial project. The Tribe rejects charges that the M.R.S. program constitutes "environmental racism," a concept that implies that the Tribe is incapable of making its own informed decisions.

Editor's Note: In the early 1990s, the Skull Valley Goshutes accepted a $100,000 Department of Energy (DOE) grant to study the feasibility of hosting a Monitored Retrieval Storage (M.R.S.) facility. The proposed facility, which would be capable of housing up to 10,000 tons of spent nuclear fuel rods (uranium), would only be temporary; a permanent repository to be built in Nevada's Yucca Mountain is in the planning stages. In 1992, the tribe reported on Phase I of the study and entered Phase IIA (receiving an additional $200,000), the favorable results of which were reported in 1993. Since that time, the Tribe has applied to the DOE to enter the third phase (IIB), which is worth $300,000 and is the last hurdle before the Tribe can build the $500 million plant that is expected to create 2,500 construction jobs and 500 permanent jobs, and to provide between $14 million and $22 million a year in revenue for the Tribe.

Skull Valley Goshute Tribe Executive Office, "'Taa-Pai' Phase IIA Report: A Comparison of Utah Waste Facilities to the Taa-Pai Industrial Park," 1993. Reprinted with permission.

*Truth is like a turtle crawling slowly over the sands of time, spreading her message to all who will listen. Rumor flies on the wings of a dove, spreading poison on smiles that glisten.*

*—author unknown*

Approximately 80 miles southwest of Salt Lake City, Utah, is located the Skull Valley Goshute Reservation. These 18,000 acres of low foothills and desert sagebrush are all that remains of an area which once stretched from the Wasatch Front into Wells, Nevada. Today, the small village on the Reservation has less than twenty families.

## Defense cutbacks

The current Reservation employers are the Tekoi Rocket Test facility and the Pony Express Station (the Tribal Store). Hercules Aerospace tests rocket engines for America's strategic defense systems on the Reservation. With the cutbacks in defense, Hercules may no longer continue to test rocket engines. The Tribe is uncertain whether or not an agreement will be reached to renew the lease of the Tribal owned Tekoi facility in 1995.[1]

Like our neighbors in Dugway, Tooele, Magna, Brigham City and nationwide, we are affected by the loss of defense jobs. For too long we have been economically dependent on the arms race. Quite unlike corporate America whose main motive in the arms race was greed, we have depended on the testing of rocket engines for economic survival.

*The charges of "environmental racism". . . smack of patronism. This attitude implies we are not intelligent enough to make our own business and environmental decisions.*

Some of our members will be affected by the loss of jobs at the Tooele Army Depot. Other members will be affected by the loss of jobs if the Tekoi Rocket Test Facility is shut down. Hercules, which has laid off close to half of its work force, has also reduced security jobs on the Reservation.[2]

The uncertainty in the defense sector of the national economy has forced change. The Tribe decided to find alternatives to Hercules Aerospace and the testing of rocket engines. The Pony Express Station (the Tribal Store), Dugway Proving Grounds and the Tooele Army Depot all combined account for the majority of Tribal employment.

## Soliciting business

We have reviewed so many businesses. It seemed that every businessman who had ever failed at anything or simply wanted the Tribe to take the financial risk on some very speculative venture approached us. In this capacity we learned a great deal about the waste industries. We have been approached to be the site for municipal solid waste sludge from New York and New Jersey. Others wanted an experimental hazardous waste incinerator to be funded by the Tribe. Others wanted the Reservation to be the site for a rock salt dump, a byproduct of a mining plant. Another "deal" was for the Tribe to fund one half of the purchase of a lumber/hardware store in return for an individual to manage the project on behalf of himself and the Tribe. Probably the silliest business project was a defunct defense contractor who wanted the Tribe to purchase his business if he relocated on the Reservation.[3]

There were others. The businessmen who had been criminally convicted and had creditors and/or banks chasing them wanted us to be their salvation and reward for the numerous years of dishonesty and failure.

---

*If it was not for the media misinformation and hysteria, the dollar value of this industrial project would be considerably less.*

---

When we first saw the M.R.S. [Monitored Retrieval Storage program] proposal we thought it was a scam, just like all of the numerous other get-rich-quick schemes and scams we'd encountered. After careful investigation we concluded that there is no conspiracy between the nuclear energy industry and the Department of Energy. There is gross, if not criminal, mismanagement of the defense nuclear waste sites around the country [causing radiological damage to these areas]. And there is a potential breach of contract looming between the Department of Energy and the nuclear energy industry[4] [because the DOE has broken its promise to dispose of the industry's nuclear waste].

We have continued to solicit businesses to come on to the Reservation. Since some of these negotiations are ongoing and therefore confidential, suffice it to say that large Fortune 500 companies have contacted the Tribe about locating in Utah.[5]

The charges of "environmental racism" and the need to "protect" and "save" us smack of patronism. This attitude implies we are not intelligent enough to make our own business and environmental decisions.

## Government as business partner

Unlike corporate executives who try to manage utility industries and have at best forty years of experience, we have a long history of business deals with the U.S. Government. First time shame on them. Second time shame on us. We clearly understand the frustration of corporate executives who need to make long-term business decisions with a partner that changes the deal *after* it has been signed and acted upon. The utility companies, like the Indian community, have the continual misfortune of new U.S. Government administrations who *will* change policy which will affect their long-term business decisions.

It is not that this ubiquitous Government can't be trusted. It is simply that when a new administration comes to power, the new administrators change the policies of the old administrators. This creates an atmosphere of uncertainty and doubt. Utility companies and Tribes like to plan for longer than four years. We need to learn patience. Four years is a very short period of time. It can take longer than four years to build power plants to generate electricity or locate a suitable business for a Reservation.

Because of the commonality of interests in long-term planning and the credibility which exists with business partners we can trust, we have decided to apply for a Phase IIB grant to study the environmental and social consequences of building a temporary storage facility for spent nuclear fuel rods to world class standards on the Taa-Pai Industrial Park within the boundaries of the Skull Valley Goshute Reservation.*

The Skull Valley Goshute Taa-Pai Industrial Park currently has two businesses, the Tekoi Rocket Test Facility and the Pony Express Station. If negotiations are successful, the credibility of the partners checks out and the numbers make sense, other businesses will be located in Skull Valley.

## Nuclear hysteria

Having thoroughly examined the storage of nuclear fuel rods in other countries we know this project is much safer than many industrial projects we have examined and more dangerous than others. The hysteria which surrounds the words "nuclear" and "radiation" will clearly make the world's most expensive storage facility unpopular with certain people and organizations who have this altruistic need to "save" us. We know that informed decisions which are in the best interests of our people and are made with their consent will not always be popular with *everyone*. Leadership is not a popularity contest.

Having studied the issue and understanding it, we are thankful for the media hype and hysteria. If it was not for the media misinformation and hysteria, the dollar value of this industrial project would be considerably less.[6] Let's be serious for a moment and realize that the nerve gas incinerator and dump out at the Tooele South Area is at least 1,000 times more dangerous than this temporary storage facility could ever hope to be.[7]

A temporary storage facility for spent fuel rods is not a "nuclear waste dump." Each fuel rod assembly costs over $750,000.00. A new Congress might again decide reprocessing [rather than storing] is in the nation's best interest. The price of uranium might increase. The nation's repository at Yucca Mountain, Nevada, or elsewhere might be completed. Twenty years is a long time. Forty years is even longer. These casks which cost over $500,000 per cask are built to last hundreds of years and safely contain all of the radiation.[8]

The decision to go into Phase IIB is not a decision to build an unsafe facility. Tooele County and the State of Utah stand to potentially benefit considerably from this project. They also assume the risks from transportation accidents and site accidents. Because this project is well over $1.5 billion in steel and concrete and creates over 500 permanent jobs, we will insist that only Utah companies to the fullest extent possible provide the material and employment.

---

*A temporary storage facility for spent fuel rods is not a "nuclear waste dump."*

---

From the interim spent-fuel storage facilities we toured in Japan, France, Britain, Sweden and on-site storage facilities in this country, we are clearly convinced that the M.R.S. can be a safe industrial project. However, like all decisions, this is a choice. We also understand that this is America. Our workplace will be as safe as we make it. All of us who work in blue-collar industries are aware of someone who at one time or another was injured on the job. Some permanently, others were down for a while. The real behaviors which exist in the American workplace are not always

the best. The recent Wilbern Mine disaster [a 1984 mine-shaft fire claiming the lives of several workers] with the quick tragedy being inflicted
upon Carbon County families reminds us of just how dangerous the Utah
workplace really can become. Each year thousands of Utahns and hundreds of thousands of Americans are injured in the workplace. Every industry is as safe or as dangerous as the people who operate it.

The future and safety of the Tribal members, especially the children,
is involved in the safety of this facility. We will not tolerate anything less
than the best labor and technology on the planet for this industrial project. If anyone has a problem with this policy we suggest they provide
their shoddy materials, bad manners and/or poor labor habits to someone
else.

In Phase IIB we will further study the site specific environmental effects and best designs for this project. Under the 1982 Nuclear Waste Policy Act and the 1987 Amendments [which provide that states or Tribes affected by a proposed nuclear waste facility may notify Congress of
"disapproval with respect to such site" (Sec 146.[a])], we reserve the right
to cancel this project at any time if we deem it in the best interest of the
Tribe.

## *Notes*

1. Conversation with Mr. Leon D. Bear, Secretary/Treasurer for the Skull
   Valley Goshute Tribe, July 19, 1993.

2. Ib. July 19, 1993.

3. Tribal Attorney, Danny Quintana, July 19, 1993. "Apparently, selling
   overpriced equipment to the Indians or locating a dump on Reservations
   is still accepted behavior in the minds of some businessmen. We were
   born in the night. But it was not last night. As we explained to our friends
   with the Edison Electric Institute, we are street smart from Salt Lake City.
   If someone can con us let them try. The problem is we have important
   work to do. We are tired of people trying to con us with their stupid
   scams and get rich quick schemes."

4. See "Nuclear Natives, The Proposed Storage of High Level Nuclear Waste
   on Native American Reservations," Phase I Report of the Skull Valley
   Goshute Tribe, 1992.

5. Tribal Attorney, Danny Quintana, July 19, 1993.

6. One television station quoted our Tribal Attorney off the record, dis-
   played the wrong Reservation and had 55-gallon drums with radioactive
   signs "NUCLEAR WASTE DUMP ON THE SKULL VALLEY GOSHUTE
   RESERVATION." One alternative news source had their facts so wrong on
   their attempt to slam the Tribe, that rather than respond we let the misinformation stand on its own merits.

7. Interview with Mr. Jack McCord, nuclear engineer and transportation expert, in Las Vegas, Nevada, on April 27, 1993.

8. The information on the casks comes from the nuclear energy industry
   and the Department of Energy. Again, because of the importance of
   safety on this project all of this information will be thoroughly checked
   out by independent sources.

\*    Taa-Pai is Light in Goshute.

# 6

# Government Should Work to Ensure Environmental Justice

## Robert Bullard

*Robert Bullard is Ware professor of Sociology and director of the Environmental Justice Resource Center in Atlanta, Georgia. His 1990 book* Dumping in Dixie: Race, Class, and Environmental Equity *is regarded as one of the founding studies indicating that environmental hazards disproportionally affect communities of color. Bullard has been active in the environmental justice movement, attending conferences and writing extensively on the issues of environmental racism and the need for remedial action. The following is an excerpt from his book* Worst Things First? The Debate over Risk-Based National Environmental Priorities.

Government should take five steps to ensure environmental justice. First, national legislation, modeled on past civil rights acts, should make illegal any environmental practices that disproportionately harm minorities. Second, environmental threats should be eliminated so that harms can be prevented before they occur. Third, in legal efforts to achieve environmental justice, the burden of proof of discrimination should be shifted from minority communities to polluting industries. Fourth, the current legal standard of "intent"—which requires the complainant in an environmental discrimination case to prove that the polluting company's discrimination was intentional—should be eliminated. Fifth, governments should redress inequities by targeting resources to communities with the worst problems. These five principles constitute a framework for environmental justice that will benefit people of color nationwide.

To end unequal environmental protection, governments should adopt five principles of environmental justice: guaranteeing the right to environmental protection, preventing harm before it occurs, shifting the burden of proof to the polluters, obviating proof of intent to discrimi-

Robert D. Bullard, "Overcoming Racism in Environmental Decision Making," *Environment*, May 1994. Adapted from the book *Worst Things First? The Debate over Risk-Based National Environmental Priorities*, published by Resources for the Future, Washington, D.C. Reprinted by permission of the publisher and the author.

nate, and redressing existing inequities.

Every individual has a right to be protected from environmental degradation. Protecting this right will require enacting a federal "fair environmental protection act." The act could be modeled after the various federal civil rights acts that have promoted nondiscrimination—with the ultimate goal of achieving "zero tolerance"—in such areas as housing, education, and employment. The act ought to address both the intended and unintended effects of public policies and industrial practices that have a disparate impact on racial and ethnic minorities and other vulnerable groups. The precedents for this framework are the Civil Rights Act of 1964, which attempted to address both de jure and de facto school segregation, the Fair Housing Act of 1968, the same act as amended in 1988, and the Voting Rights Act of 1965.

---

*Every individual has a right to be protected from environmental degradation.*

---

For the first time in the agency's 23-year history, EPA's Office of Civil Rights has begun investigating charges of environmental discrimination under Title VI of the 1964 Civil Rights Act. The cases involve waste facility siting disputes in Michigan, Alabama, Mississippi, and Louisiana. Similarly, in September 1993, the U.S. Civil Rights Commission issued a report entitled *The Battle for Environmental Justice in Louisiana: Government, Industry, and the People.* This report confirmed what most people who live in "Cancer Alley"—the 85-mile stretch along the Mississippi River from Baton Rouge to New Orleans—already knew: African American communities along the Mississippi River bear disproportionate health burdens from industrial pollution.[1]

A number of bills have been introduced into Congress that address some aspect of environmental justice:

- The "Environmental Justice Act of 1993" (H.R. 2105) would provide the federal government with the statistical documentation and ranking of the top 100 "environmental high impact areas" that warrant attention.
- The "Environmental Equal Rights Act of 1993" (H.R. 1924) seeks to amend the Solid Waste Act and would prevent waste facilities from being sited in "environmentally disadvantaged communities."
- The "Environmental Health Equity Information Act of 1993" (H.R. 1925) seeks to amend the Comprehensive Environmental Response, Compensation, and Liability Act of 1990 (CERCLA) to require the Agency for Toxic Substances and Disease Registry to collect and maintain information on the race, age, gender, ethnic origin, income level, and educational level of persons living in communities adjacent to toxic substance contamination.
- The "Waste Export and Import Prohibition Act" (H.R. 3706) would ban waste exports as of 1 July 1994 to countries that are not members of the Organization for Economic Cooperation and Development (OECD); the bill would also ban waste exports to and imports from OECD countries as of 1 January 1999.

The states are also beginning to address environmental justice concerns. Arkansas and Louisiana were the first two to enact environmental justice laws. Virginia has passed a legislative resolution on environmental justice. California, Georgia, New York, North Carolina, and South Carolina have pending legislation to address environmental disparities.

Environmental justice groups have succeeded in getting President Clinton to act on the problem of unequal environmental protection, an issue that has been buried for more than three decades. On 11 February 1994, Clinton signed an executive order entitled "Federal Actions to Address Environmental Justice in Minority Populations and Low-Income Populations." This new executive order reinforces what has been law since the passage of the 1964 Civil Rights Act, which prohibits discriminatory practices in programs receiving federal financial assistance.

The executive order also refocuses attention on the National Environmental Policy Act of 1970 (NEPA), which established national policy goals for the protection, maintenance, and enhancement of the environment. The express goal of NEPA is to ensure for all U.S. citizens a safe, healthful, productive, and aesthetically and culturally pleasing environment. NEPA requires federal agencies to prepare detailed statements on the environmental effects of proposed federal actions significantly affecting the quality of human health. Environmental impact statements prepared under NEPA have routinely downplayed the social impacts of federal projects on racial and ethnic minorities and low-income groups.

Under the new executive order, federal agencies and other institutions that receive federal monies have a year to implement an environmental justice strategy. For these strategies to be effective, agencies must move away from the "DAD" (decide, announce, and defend) modus operandi. EPA cannot address all of the environmental injustices alone but must work in concert with other stakeholders, such as state and local governments and private industry. A new interagency approach might include the following:

- Grassroots environmental justice groups and their networks must become full partners, not silent or junior partners, in planning the implementation of the new executive order.
- An advisory commission should include representatives of environmental justice, civil rights, legal, labor, and public health groups, as well as the relevant governmental agencies, to advise on the implementation of the executive order.
- State and regional education, training, and outreach forums and workshops on implementing the executive order should be organized.
- The executive order should become part of the agenda of national conferences and meetings of elected officials, civil rights and environmental groups, public health and medical groups, educators, and other professional organizations.

The executive order comes at an important juncture in this nation's history: Few communities are willing to welcome LULUs [locally undesirable land uses such as landfills, incinerators, sewage treatment plants, and other noxious facilities] or to become dumping grounds for other people's garbage, toxic waste, or industrial pollution. In the real world, however, if a community happens to be poor and inhabited by persons of color, it is likely to suffer from a "double whammy" of unequal protection and elevated health threats. This is unjust and illegal.

The civil rights and environmental laws of the land must be enforced even if it means the loss of a few jobs. This argument was a sound one in the 1860s, when the 13th Amendment to the Constitution, which freed the slaves in the United States, was passed over the opposition of pro-slavery advocates who posited that the new law would create unemployment (slaves had a zero unemployment rate), drive up wages, and inflict undue hardship on the plantation economy.

## Prevention of harm

Prevention, the elimination of the threat before harm occurs, should be the preferred strategy of governments. For example, to solve the [problem of lead poisoning in children due to lead-based paint in old houses], the primary focus should be shifted from treating children who have been poisoned to eliminating the threat by removing lead from houses.

Overwhelming scientific evidence exists on the ill effects of lead on the human body. However, very little action has been taken to rid the nation's housing of lead even though lead poisoning is a preventable disease tagged the "number one environmental health threat to children."[2]

Lead began to be phased out of gasoline in the 1970s. It is ironic that the "regulations were initially developed to protect the newly developed catalytic converter in automobiles, a pollution-control device that happens to be rendered inoperative by lead, rather than to safeguard human health."[3] In 1971, a child was not considered "at risk" unless he or she had 40 micrograms of lead per deciliter of blood ($\mu$g/dl). Since that time, the amount of lead that is considered safe has continually dropped. In 1991, the U.S. Public Health Service changed the official definition of an unsafe level to 10 $\mu$g/dl. Even at that level, a child's IQ can be slightly diminished and physical growth stunted.

Lead poisoning is correlated with both income and race. In 1988, the Agency for Toxic Substances and Disease Registry found that, among families earning less than $6,000, 68 percent of African American children had lead poisoning, as opposed to 36 percent of white children.[4] In families with incomes exceeding $15,000, more than 38 percent of African American children suffered from lead poisoning, compared with 12 percent of white children. Thus, even when differences in income are taken into account, middle-class African American children are three times more likely to be poisoned with lead than are their middle-class white counterparts.

A 1990 report by the Environmental Defense Fund estimated that, under the 1991 standard of 10 $\mu$g/dl, 96 percent of African American children and 80 percent of white children of poor families who live in inner cities have unsafe amounts of lead in their blood—amounts sufficient to reduce IQ somewhat, harm hearing, reduce the ability to concentrate, and stunt physical growth.[5] Even in families with annual incomes greater than $15,000, 85 percent of urban African American children have unsafe lead levels, compared to 47 percent of white children.

In the spring of 1991, the Bush administration announced an ambitious program to reduce lead exposure of children, including widespread testing of homes, certification of those who remove lead from homes, and medical treatment for affected children. Six months later, the Centers for Disease Control announced that the administration "does not see this as a necessary federal role to legislate or regulate the cleanup of lead poisoning, to require that homes be tested, to require home owners to disclose results once they are known, or to establish standards for those who test or clean up lead hazards."[6]

According to the *New York Times*, the National Association of Realtors pressured President Bush to drop his lead initiative because they feared that forcing homeowners to eliminate lead hazards would add from $5,000 to $10,000 to the price of those homes, further harming a real estate market already devastated by the aftershocks of Reaganomics.[7] The public debate has pitted real estate and housing interests against public health interests. Right now, the housing interests appear to be winning.

For more than two decades, Congress and the nation's medical and public health establishments have waffled, procrastinated, and shuffled papers while the lead problem steadily grows worse. During the years of President Reagan's "benign neglect," funding dropped very low. Even in the best years, when funding has risen to as much as $50 million per year, it has never reached levels that would make a real dent in the problem.

Much could be done to protect at-risk populations if the current laws were enforced. For example, a lead smelter operated for 50 years in a predominately African American West Dallas neighborhood, where it caused extreme health problems for nearby residents. Dallas officials were informed as early as 1972 that lead from three lead smelters was finding its way into the bloodstreams of children who lived in two mostly African American and Latino neighborhoods: West Dallas and East Oak Cliff.[8]

---

*If a community happens to be poor and inhabited by persons of color, it is likely to suffer from a "double whammy" of unequal protection and elevated health threats.*

---

Living near the RSR and Dixie Metals smelters was associated with a 36-percent increase in childhood blood lead levels. The city was urged to restrict the emissions of lead into the atmosphere and to undertake a large screening program to determine the extent of the public health problem. The city failed to take immediate action to protect the residents who lived near the smelters.

In 1980, EPA, informed about possible health risks associated with the Dallas lead smelters, commissioned another lead-screening study. This study confirmed what was already known a decade earlier: Children living near the Dallas smelters were likely to have greater lead concentrations in their blood than children who did not live near the smelters.[9]

The city only took action after the local newspapers published a series of headline-grabbing stories in 1983 on the "potentially dangerous" lead levels discovered by EPA researchers in 1981.[10] The articles triggered widespread concern, public outrage, several class-action lawsuits, and legal action by the Texas attorney general.

Although EPA was armed with a wealth of scientific data on the West Dallas lead problem, the agency chose to play politics with the community by scrapping a voluntary plan offered by RSR to clean up the "hot spots" in the neighborhood. John Hernandez, EPA's deputy administrator, blocked the cleanup and called for yet another round of tests to be designed by the Centers for Disease Control with EPA and the Dallas Health Department. The results of the new study were released in February 1983. Again, this study established the smelter as the source of elevated lead levels in West Dallas children.[11] Hernandez's delay of cleanup actions in West Dallas was tantamount to waiting for a body count.[12]

After years of delay, the West Dallas plaintiffs negotiated an out-of-court settlement worth more than $45 million. The lawsuit was settled in June 1983 as RSR agreed to pay for cleaning up the soil in West Dallas, a blood-testing program for children and pregnant women, and the installation of new antipollution equipment. The settlement was made on behalf of 370 children—almost all of whom were poor, black residents of the West Dallas public housing project—and 40 property owners. The agreement was one of the largest community lead-contamination settlements ever awarded in the United States.[13] The settlement, however, did not require the smelter to close. Moreover, the pollution equipment for the smelter was never installed.

In May 1984, however, the Dallas Board of Adjustments, a city agency responsible for monitoring land-use violations, asked the city attorney to close the smelter permanently for violating the city's zoning code. The lead smelter had operated in the mostly African American West Dallas neighborhood for 50 years without having the necessary use permits. Just four months later, the West Dallas smelter was permanently closed. After repeated health citations, fines, and citizens' complaints against the smelter, one has to question the city's lax enforcement of health and land-use regulations in African American and Latino neighborhoods.

The smelter is now closed. Although an initial cleanup was carried out in 1984, the lead problem has not gone away.[14] On 31 December 1991, EPA crews began a cleanup of the West Dallas neighborhood. It is estimated that the crews will remove between 30,000 and 40,000 cubic yards of lead-contaminated soil from several West Dallas sites, including school property and about 140 private homes. The project will cost EPA from $3 million to $4 million. The lead content of the soil collected from dump sites in the neighborhood ranged from 8,060 to 21,000 parts per million.[15] Under federal standards, levels of 500 to 1,000 parts per million are considered hazardous. In April 1993, the entire West Dallas neighborhood was declared a Superfund site.

There have been a few other signs related to the lead issue that suggest a consensus on environmental justice is growing among coalitions of environmental, social justice, and civil libertarian groups. The Natural Resources Defense Council, the National Association for the Advancement of Colored People Legal Defense and Education Fund, the American Civil Liberties Union, and the Legal Aid Society of Alameda County joined forces and won an out-of-court settlement worth between $15 million and $20 million for a blood-testing program in California. The lawsuit (*Matthews v. Coye*) arose because the state of California was not performing the federally mandated testing of some 557,000 poor children who receive Medicaid. This historic agreement will likely trigger similar actions in other states that have failed to perform federally mandated screening.[16]

Lead screening is important but it is not the solution. New government-mandated lead abatement initiatives are needed. The nation needs a "Lead Superfund" cleanup program. Public health should not be sacrificed even in a sluggish housing market. Surely, if termite inspections (required in both booming and sluggish housing markets) can be mandated to protect individual home investment, a lead-free home can be mandated to protect human health. Ultimately, the lead debate—public health (who is affected) versus property rights (who pays for cleanup)—is a value conflict that will not be resolved by the scientific community.

## Shift the burden of proof

Under the current system, individuals who challenge polluters must prove that they have been harmed, discriminated against, or disproportionately affected. Few poor or minority communities have the resources to hire the lawyers, expert witnesses, and doctors needed to sustain such a challenge. Thus, the burden of proof must be shifted to the polluters who do harm, discriminate, or do not give equal protection to minorities and other overburdened classes.

Environmental justice would require the entities that are applying for operating permits for landfills, incinerators, smelters, refineries, and chemical plants, for example, to prove that their operations are not harmful to human health, will not disproportionately affect minorities or the poor, and are nondiscriminatory.

A case in point is Louisiana Energy Services' proposal to build the nation's first privately owned uranium enrichment plant. The proposed plant would handle about 17 percent of the estimated U.S. requirement for enrichment services in the year 2000. Clearly, the burden of proof should be on Louisiana Energy Services, the state government, and the Nuclear Regulatory Commission to demonstrate that local residents' rights would not be violated in permitting the plant. At present, the burden of proof is on local residents to demonstrate that their health would be endangered and their community adversely affected by the plant.

According to the Nuclear Regulatory Commission's 1993 draft environmental impact statement, the proposed site for the facility is Claiborne Parish, Louisiana, which has a per-capita income of only $5,800 per year—just 45 percent of the national average.[17] The enrichment plant would be just one-quarter mile from the almost wholly African American community of Center Springs, founded in 1910, and one and one-quarter miles from Forest Grove, which was founded by freed slaves. However, the draft statement describes the socioeconomic and community characteristics of Homer, a town that is five miles from the proposed site and whose population is more than 50 percent white, rather than those of Center Springs or Forest Grove. As far as the draft is concerned, the communities of Center Springs and Forest Grove do not exist; they are invisible.

The racial composition of Claiborne Parish is 53.43 percent white, 46.09 percent African American, 0.16 percent American Indian, 0.07 percent Asian, 0.23 percent Hispanic, and 0.01 percent "other."[18] Thus, the parish's percentage population of African Americans is nearly four times that of the nation and nearly one and one-half times that of Louisiana. (African Americans composed 12 percent of the U.S. population and 29 percent of Louisiana's population in 1990.)

Clearly, Claiborne Parish's current residents would receive fewer of the plant's potential benefits—high-paying jobs, home construction, and an increased tax base—than would those who moved into the area or commuted to it to work at the facility. An increasing number of migrants will take jobs at the higher end of the skill and pay scale. These workers are expected to buy homes outside of the parish. Residents of Claiborne

Parish, on the other hand, are likely to get the jobs at the lower end of the skill and pay scale.[19]

Ultimately, the plant's social costs would be borne by nearby residents, while the benefits would be more dispersed. The potential social costs include increased noise and traffic, threats to public safety and to mental and physical health, and LULUs.

The case of Richmond, California, provides more evidence of the need to shift the burden of proof. A 1989 study, *Richmond at Risk*, found that the African American residents of this city bear the brunt of toxic releases in Contra Costa County and the San Francisco Bay area.[20] At least 38 industrial sites in and around the city store up to 94 million pounds of 45 different chemicals, including ammonia, chlorine, hydrogen fluoride, and nitric acid. However, the burden of proof is on Richmond residents to show that they are harmed by nearby toxic releases.

On 26 July 1993, sulfur trioxide escaped from the General Chemical plant in Richmond, where people of color make up a majority of the residents. More than 20,000 citizens were sent to the hospital. A September 1993 report by the Bay Area Air Quality Management District confirmed that "the operation was conducted in a negligent manner without due regard to the potential consequences of a miscalculation or equipment malfunction, and without required permits from the District."[21]

---

*The civil rights and environmental laws of the land must be enforced even if it means the loss of a few jobs.*

---

When Richmond residents protested the planned expansion of a Chevron refinery, they were asked to prove that they had been harmed by Chevron's operation. Recently, public pressure has induced Chevron to set aside $4.2 million to establish a new health clinic and help the surrounding community.

A third case involves conditions surrounding the 1,900 *maquiladoras*, assembly plants operated by U.S., Japanese, and other countries' companies along the 2,000-mile U.S.-Mexican border.[22] A 1983 agreement between the United States and Mexico requires U.S. companies in Mexico to export their waste products to the United States, and plants must notify EPA when they are doing so. However, a 1986 survey of 772 maquiladoras revealed that only 20 of the plants informed EPA when they were exporting waste to the United States, even though 86 percent of the plants used toxic chemicals in their manufacturing processes. And in 1989, only 10 waste shipment notices were filed with EPA.[23]

Much of the waste from the maquiladoras is illegally dumped in sewers, ditches, and the desert. All along the Rio Grande, plants dump toxic wastes into the river, from which 95 percent of the region's residents get their drinking water. In the border cities of Brownsville, Texas, and Matamoros, Mexico, the rate of anencephaly—being born without a brain—is four times the U.S. national average.[24] Affected families have filed lawsuits against 88 of the area's 100 maquiladoras for exposing the community to xylene, a cleaning solvent that can cause brain hemorrhages and lung and kidney damage. However, as usual, the burden of proof rests with the victims. Unfortunately, Mexico's environmental regulatory agency is understaffed and ill-equipped to enforce the country's environmental laws adequately.

## Obviate proof of intent

Laws must allow disparate impact and statistical weight—as opposed to "intent"—to infer discrimination because proving intentional or purposeful discrimination in a court of law is next to impossible. The first lawsuit to charge environmental discrimination in the placement of a waste facility, *Bean v. Southwestern Waste,* was filed in 1979. The case involved residents of Houston's Northwood Manor, a suburban, middle-class neighborhood of homeowners, and Browning-Ferris Industries, a private disposal company based in Houston.

More than 83 percent of the residents in the subdivision owned their single-family, detached homes. Thus, the Northwood Manor neighborhood was an unlikely candidate for a municipal landfill except that, in 1978, it was more than 82 percent black. An earlier attempt had been made to locate a municipal landfill in the same general area in 1970, when the subdivision and local school district had a majority white population. The 1970 landfill proposal was killed by the Harris County Board of Supervisors as being an incompatible land use; the site was deemed to be too close to a residential area and a neighborhood school. In 1978, however, the controversial sanitary landfill was built only 1,400 feet from a high school, football stadium, track field, and the North Forest Independent School District's administration building.[25] Because Houston has been and continues to be highly segregated, few Houstonians are unaware of where the African American neighborhoods end and the white ones begin. In 1970, for example, more than 90 percent of the city's African American residents lived in mostly black areas. By 1980, 82 percent of Houston's African American population lived in mostly black areas.[26]

Houston is the only major U.S. city without zoning. In 1992, the city council voted to institute zoning, but the measure was defeated at the polls in 1993. The city's African American neighborhoods have paid a high price for the city's unrestrained growth and lack of a zoning policy. Black Houston was allowed to become the dumping ground for the city's garbage. In every case, the racial composition of Houston's African American neighborhoods had been established before the waste facilities were sited.[27]

From the early 1920s through the late 1970s, all five of the city-owned sanitary landfills and six out of eight of Houston's municipal solid waste incinerators were located in mostly African American neighborhoods.[28] The other two incinerator sites were located in a Latino neighborhood and a white neighborhood. One of the oldest waste sites in Houston was located in Freedmen's Town, an African American neighborhood settled by former slaves in the 1860s. The site has since been built over with a charity hospital and a low-income public housing project.

Private industry took its lead from the siting pattern established by the city government. From 1970 to 1978, three of the four privately owned landfills used to dispose of Houston's garbage were located in mostly African American neighborhoods. The fourth privately owned landfill, which was sited in 1971, was located in the mostly white Chattwood subdivision. A residential park or "buffer zone" separates the white neighborhood from the landfill. Both government and industry responded to white neighborhood associations and their NIMBY (not in my backyard) organizations by siting LULUs according to the PIBBY (place in blacks' backyards) strategy.[29]

The statistical evidence in *Bean v. Southwestern Waste* overwhelmingly supported the disproportionate impact argument. Overall, 14 of the 17 (82 percent) solid waste facilities used to dispose of Houston's garbage were located in mostly African American neighborhoods. Considering that Houston's African American residents comprised only 28 percent of the city's total population, they clearly were forced to bear a disproportionate burden of the city's solid waste facilities.[30] However, the federal judge ruled against the plaintiffs on the grounds that "purposeful discrimination" was not demonstrated.

Although the Northwood Manor residents lost their lawsuit, they did influence the way the Houston city government and the state of Texas addressed race and waste facility siting. Acting under intense pressure from the African American community, the Houston city council passed a resolution in 1980 that prohibited city-owned trucks from dumping at the controversial landfill. In 1981, the Houston city council passed an ordinance restricting the construction of solid waste disposal sites near public facilities such as schools. And the Texas Department of Health updated its requirements of landfill permit applicants to include detailed land-use, economic, and sociodemographic data on areas where they proposed to site landfills. Black Houstonians had sent a clear signal to the Texas Department of Health, the city of Houston, and private disposal companies that they would fight any future attempts to place waste disposal facilities in their neighborhoods.

Since *Bean v. Southwestern Waste*, not a single landfill or incinerator has been sited in an African American neighborhood in Houston. Not until nearly a decade after that suit did environmental discrimination resurface in the courts. A number of recent cases have challenged siting decisions using the environmental discrimination argument: *East Bibb Twiggs Neighborhood Association v. Macon-Bibb County Planning & Zoning Commission* (1989), *Bordeaux Action Committee v. Metro Government of Nashville* (1990), *R.I.S.E. v. Kay* (1991), and *El Pueblo para El Aire y Agua Limpio v. County of Kings* (1991). Unfortunately, these legal challenges are also confronted with the test of demonstrating "purposeful" discrimination.

## Redress inequities

Disproportionate impacts must be redressed by targeting action and resources. Resources should be spent where environmental and health problems are greatest, as determined by some ranking scheme—but one not limited to risk assessment. EPA already has geographic targeting that involves selecting a physical area, often a naturally defined area such as a watershed; assessing the condition of the natural resources and range of environmental threats, including risks to public health; formulating and implementing integrated, holistic strategies for restoring or protecting living resources and their habitats within that area; and evaluating the progress of those strategies toward their objectives.[31]

Relying solely on proof of a cause-and-effect relationship as defined by traditional epidemiology disguises the exploitative way the polluting industries have operated in some communities and condones a passive acceptance of the status quo.[32] Because it is difficult to establish causation, polluting industries have the upper hand. They can always hide behind "science" and demand "proof" that their activities are harmful to humans or the environment.

A 1992 EPA report, *Securing Our Legacy*, described the agency's geographic initiatives as "protecting what we love."[33] The strategy emphasizes "pollution prevention, multimedia enforcement, research into causes and cures of environmental stress, stopping habitat loss, education, and constituency building."[34] Examples of geographic initiatives under way include the Chesapeake Bay, Great Lakes, Gulf of Mexico, and Mexican Border programs.

Such targeting should channel resources to the hot spots, communities that are burdened with more than their fair share of environmental problems. For example, EPA's Region VI has developed geographic information system and comparative risk methodologies to evaluate environmental equity concerns in the region. The methodology combines susceptibility factors, such as age, pregnancy, race, income, pre-existing disease, and lifestyle, with chemical release data from the Toxic Release Inventory and monitoring information; state health department vital statistics data; and geographic and demographic data—especially from areas around hazardous waste sites—for its regional equity assessment.

Region VI's 1992 Gulf Coast Toxics Initiatives project is an outgrowth of its equity assessment. The project targets facilities on the Texas and Louisiana coast, a "sensitive . . . eco-region where most of the releases in the five-state region occur."[35] Inspectors will spend 38 percent of their time in this "multimedia enforcement effort."[36] It is not clear how this percentage was determined, but, for the project to move beyond the "first-step" phase and begin addressing real inequities, most of its resources (not just inspectors) must be channeled to the areas where most of the problems occur.

> *The lessons from the civil rights struggles . . . suggest that environmental justice requires a legislative foundation.*

A 1993 EPA study of Toxic Release Inventory data from Louisiana's petrochemical corridor found that "populations within two miles of facilities releasing 90% of total industrial corridor air releases feature a higher proportion of minorities than the state average; facilities releasing 88% have a higher proportion than the Industrial Corridor parishes' average.[37]

To no one's surprise, communities in Corpus Christi, neighborhoods that run along the Houston Ship Channel and petrochemical corridor, and many unincorporated communities along the 85-mile stretch of the Mississippi River from Baton Rouge to New Orleans ranked at or near the top in terms of pollution discharges in EPA Region VI's Gulf Coast Toxics Initiatives equity assessment. It is very likely that similar rankings would be achieved using the environmental justice framework. However, the question that remains is one of resource allocation—the level of resources that Region VI will channel into solving the pollution problem in communities that have a disproportionately large share of poor people, working-class people, and people of color.

Health concerns raised by Louisiana's residents and grassroots activists in such communities as Alsen, St. Gabriel, Geismer, Morrisonville, and Lions—all of which are located in close proximity to polluting industries—have not been adequately addressed by local parish supervisors, state environmental and health officials, or the federal and regional offices of EPA.[38]

A few contaminated African American communities in southeast Louisiana have been bought out or are in the process of being bought out by industries under their "good neighbor" programs. Moving people away from the health threat is only a partial solution, however, as long as damage to the environment continues. For example, Dow Chemical, the state's largest chemical plant, is buying out residents of mostly African American Morrisonville.[39] The communities of Sun Rise and Reveilletown, which were founded by freed slaves, have already been bought out.

Many of the community buyout settlements are sealed. The secret nature of the agreements limits public scrutiny, community comparisons, and disclosure of harm or potential harm. Few of the recent settlement agreements allow for health monitoring or surveillance of affected residents once they are dispersed.[40] Some settlements have even required the "victims" to sign waivers that preclude them from bringing any further lawsuits against the polluting industry.

## A framework for environmental justice

The solution to unequal protection lies in the realm of environmental justice for all people. No community—rich or poor, black or white—should be allowed to become a "sacrifice zone." The lessons from the civil rights struggles around housing, employment, education, and public accommodations over the past four decades suggest that environmental justice requires a legislative foundation. It is not enough to demonstrate the existence of unjust and unfair conditions; the practices that cause the conditions must be made illegal.

The five principles already described—the right to protection, prevention of harm, shifting the burden of proof, obviating proof of intent to discriminate, and targeting resources to redress inequities—constitute a framework for environmental justice. The framework incorporates a legislative strategy, modeled after landmark civil rights mandates, that would make environmental discrimination illegal and costly.

Although enforcing current laws in a nondiscriminatory way would help, a new legislative initiative is needed. Unequal protection must be attacked via a federal "fair environmental protection act" that redefines protection as a right rather than a privilege. Legislative initiatives must also be directed at states because many of the decisions and problems lie with state actions.

Noxious facility siting and cleanup decisions involve very little science and a lot of politics. Institutional discrimination exists in every social arena, including environmental decisionmaking. Burdens and benefits are not randomly distributed. Reliance solely on "objective" science for environmental decisionmaking—in a world shaped largely by power politics and special interests—often masks institutional racism. For example, the assignment of "acceptable" risk and use of "averages" often result from value judgments that serve to legitimate existing inequities. A national environmental justice framework that incorporates the five principles presented above is needed to begin addressing environmental inequities that result from procedural, geographic, and societal imbalances.

The antidiscrimination and enforcement measures called for here are no more regressive than the initiatives undertaken to eliminate slavery and segregation in the United States. Opponents argued at the time that such actions would hurt the slaves by creating unemployment and destroying black institutions, such as businesses and schools. Similar arguments were made in opposition to sanctions against the racist system of apartheid in South Africa. But people of color who live in environmental "sacrifice zones"—from migrant farm workers who are exposed to deadly pesticides to the parents of inner-city children threatened by lead poisoning—will welcome any new approaches that will reduce environmental disparities and eliminate the threats to their families' health.

## Notes

1. U.S. Commission on Civil Rights, *The Battle for Environmental Justice in Louisiana: Government, Industry, and the People* (Kansas City, Mo., 1993).

2. Agency for Toxic Substances and Disease Registry, *The Nature and Extent of Lead Poisoning in Children in the United States: A Report to Congress* (Atlanta, Ga.: U.S. Department of Health and Human Services, 1988).

3. P. Reich, *The Hour of Lead* (Washington, D.C.: Environmental Defense Fund, 1992).

4. Agency for Toxic Substances and Disease Registry, note 2 above.

5. K. Florini et al., *Legacy of Lead: America's Continuing Epidemic of Childhood Lead Poisoning* (Washington, D.C.: Environmental Defense Fund, 1990).

6. P. J. Hilts, "White House Shuns Key Role in Lead Exposure," *New York Times*, 24 August 1991, 14.

7. Ibid.

8. Dallas Alliance Environmental Task Force, *Alliance Final Report* (Dallas, Tex: Dallas Alliance, 1983).

9. J. Lash, K. Gillman, and D. Sheridan, *A Season of Spoils: The Reagan Administration's Attack on the Environment* (New York: Pantheon Books, 1984), 131-39.

10. D. W. Nauss, "EPA Official: Dallas Lead Study Misleading," *Dallas Times Herald*, 20 March 1983, 1; idem, "The People vs. the Lead Smelter," *Dallas Times Herald*, 17 July 1983, 18; B. Lodge, "EPA Official Faults Dallas Lead Smelter," *Dallas Morning News*, 20 March 1983, Al; and Lash, Gillman, and Sheridan, note 9 above.

11. U.S. Environmental Protection Agency Region VI, *Report of the Dallas Area Lead Assessment Study* (Dallas, Tex., 1983).

12. Lash, Gillman, and Sheridan, note 9 above.

13. R. D. Bullard, *Dumping in Dixie: Race, Class, and Environmental Quality* (Boulder, Colo: Westview Press, 1990).

14. S. Scott and R. L. Loftis, "Slag Sites' Health Risks Still Unclear," *Dallas Morning News*, 23 July 1991, Al.

15. Ibid.

16. B. L. Lee, "Environmental Litigation on Behalf of Poor, Minority Children: Matthews v. Coye: A Case Study" (paper presented at the Annual Meeting of the American Association for the Advancement of Science, Chicago, 9 February 1992).

17. Nuclear Regulatory Commission, *Draft Environmental Impact Statement for the Construction and Operation of Claiborne Enrichment Center, Homer, Louisiana* (Washington, D.C., 1993), 3-108.

18. See U.S. Census Bureau, *1990 Census of Population, General Population Characteristics—Louisiana* (Washington, D.C.: U.S. Government Printing Office, May 1992).

19. Nuclear Regulatory Commission, note 17 above, 4-38.

20. Citizens for a Better Environment, *Richmond at Risk* (San Francisco, Calif., 1992).

21. Bay Area Air Quality Management District, *General Chemical Incident of July 26, 1993* (San Francisco, Calif., 15 September 1993), 1.

22. R. Sanchez, "Health and Environmental Risks of the Maquiladora in Mexicali," *Natural Resources Journal* 30 (Winter 1990): 163-86.

23. Center for Investigative Reporting, *Global Dumping Grounds: The International Traffic in Hazardous Waste* (Washington, D.C.: Seven Locks Press, 1989), 59.

24. Working Group on Canada-Mexico Free Trade, "Que Pasa? A Canada-Mexico 'Free' Trade Deal," *New Solutions: A Journal of Environmental and Occupational Health Policy* 2 (1991): 10-25.

25. R. D. Bullard, "Solid Waste Sites and the Black Houston Community," *Sociological Inquiry* 53, nos. 2 and 3 (1983): 273-88.

26. R. D. Bullard, *Invisible Houston: The Black Experience in Boom and Bust* (College Station, Tex: Texas A&M University Press, 1987).

27. Bullard, 1983, 1987, and 1990, notes 13, 25, and 26 above. The unit of analysis for the Houston waste study was the neighborhood, not the census tract. The concept of neighborhood predates census tract geography, which became available only in 1950. Neighborhood studies date back nearly a century. *Neighborhood* as used here is defined as "a social/spatial unit of social organization . . . larger than a household and smaller than a city." See A. Hunter, "Urban Neighborhoods: Its Analytical and Social Contexts," *Urban Affairs Quarterly* 14 (1979): 270. The neighborhood is part of a city's geography, a place defined by specific physical boundaries and block groups. Similarly, the black neighborhood is a "highly diversified set of interrelated structures and aggregates of people who are held together by forces of white oppression and racism." See J. E. Blackwell, *The Black Community: Diversity and Unity* (New York: Harper & Row, 1985), xiii.

28. Bullard, 1983, 1987, and 1990, notes 13, 25, and 26 above.

29. Ibid.

30. Ibid.

31. U.S. Environmental Protection Agency, *Strategies and Framework for the Future: Final Report* (Washington, D.C., 1992), 12.

32. K. S. Shrader-Frechette, *Risk and Rationality: Philosophical Foundations for Populist Reform* (Berkeley, Calif.: University of California Press, 1992), 98.

33. U.S. Environmental Protection Agency, "Geographic Initiatives. Protecting What We Love," *Securing Our Legacy: An EPA Progress Report 1989-1991* (Washington, D.C., 1992), 32.

34. Ibid.

35. U.S. Environmental Protection Agency, *Environmental Equity: Reducing*

*Risk for All Communities*, vol. 2, *Supporting Documents* (Washington, D.C., 1992), 60.

36. Ibid.

37. U.S. Environmental Protection Agency, *Toxic Release Inventory & Emission Reduction 1987-1990 in the Lower Mississippi River Industrial Corridor* (Washington, D.C., 1993), 25.

38. Bullard, 1990, note 13 above; C. Beasley, "Of Pollution and Poverty: Keeping Watch in Cancer Alley," *Buzzworm* 2, no. 4 (1990): 39-45; and S. Lewis, B. Keating, and D. Russell, *Inconclusive by Design: Waste, Fraud, and Abuse in Federal Environmental Health Research* (Boston, Mass.: National Toxics Campaign, 1992).

39. J. O'Byrne, "The Death of a Town," *Times Picayune*, 20 February 1991, A1.

40. Bullard, 1990, note 13 above; J. O'Byrne and M. Schleifstein, "Invisible Poisons," *Times Picayune*, 18 February 1991, A1; and Lewis, Keating, and Russell, note 38 above.

# 7

# Environmental Justice Can Be Achieved Through Negotiated Compensation

Christopher Boerner and Thomas Lambert

*Christopher Boerner is the Jeanne and Arthur Ansehl Fellow at the Center for the Study of American Business at Washington University in St. Louis, Missouri. Thomas Lambert is the Clifford M. Hardin Fellow at the center.*

Environmental justice has become a premier environmental and civil rights issue garnering the support of Congress and President Clinton for several measures that will prohibit the siting of waste facilities in minority communities. But such attempts to legislate environmental equity are only temporarily effective at best and economically harmful to the communities they seek to protect at worst. Prohibiting siting in disadvantaged communities cannot prevent site areas from becoming populated with the poor and minorities who move to the source of pollution precisely because of lower property values; however, denying these communities the economic opportunities of new facilities offering jobs and other economic benefits would ensure that such communities remain poor and unhealthy. The only way to achieve an equitable distribution of environmental costs and benefits is to charge those benefiting from the land use while financially compensating those who host the undesirable facility. There are a variety of ways to structure the compensation process; but however it is instituted, compensation remains the only solution to environmental racism that allows the community to decide for itself.

Eliminating "environmental racism" has fast become one of the premier civil rights and environmental issues of the 1990s. Over the past 15 years, what began as a modest grassroots social movement has expanded to become a national issue, combining environmentalism's sense of urgency with the ethical concerns of the civil rights movement. According to "environmental justice" advocates, discrimination in the siting and permitting of industrial and waste facilities has forced minorities and the

Christopher Boerner and Thomas Lambert, *Environmental Justice?*, a study published by the Center for the Study of American Business, Washington University, St. Louis, Missouri. Adapted by the authors for inclusion in the present volume. Reprinted by permission of the publisher.

poor to disproportionately bear the ill-effects of pollution compared to more affluent whites. What's more, advocates contend, the discriminatory application of environmental regulations and remediation procedures has essentially let polluters in minority communities "off the hook."

To remedy this perceived imbalance, policymakers in Washington have mounted a full-court press. On February 11, 1994, the Clinton Administration issued an executive order on environmental justice, requiring federal agencies to demonstrate that their programs and policies do not unfairly inflict environmental harm on the poor and minorities. The order also creates an inter-agency task force to inform the president of all federal environmental justice policies and to work closely with the Environmental Protection Agency's Office of Environmental Equity as well as other government agencies to ensure that those policies are implemented promptly. In addition to the president's executive order, Congress is debating several separate bills designed to guarantee environmental equity. These proposals would affect the location of industrial facilities.

With charges of racism, discrimination, and social negligence being bandied about, discussions of the environmental justice issue are often passionate and, occasionally, inflammatory. Behind emotion, however, two critical questions arise: Does the existing evidence justify such a high-level commitment of resources to addressing environmental justice claims? and What reasonable steps should society take to ensure that environmental policies are fairly enacted and implemented?

Contrary to conventional wisdom, the answers to these questions are neither simple nor readily apparent. While it certainly seems noncontroversial to assert that environmental officials ought to equally enforce existing laws, the question of siting and permitting reforms is not so clear cut. Before approving additional regulations on facility siting and permitting, policy makers would be well advised to candidly assess both the quality of the existing environmental racism research and the likely costs and benefits of proposed solutions to this problem. Only with such a critical eye can legislators be certain that the measures ultimately enacted are both cost effective and successful in addressing the equity concerns of minority and low-income communities. . . .

## Responding to environmental justice claims

There may well be room for policy makers to reform environmental laws in a manner which would prevent future environmental inequities without discouraging the siting and operation of socially beneficial projects. Crafting such policies requires that one understand pollution from an economic perspective. Such an awareness gets at the very heart of the environmental justice issue and provides a theoretical framework for dealing with the perceived problem.

Economists refer to pollution as an "external cost" or a "negative externality." Pollution is negative because it is undesirable, and it is an externality because it affects those who are outside of (i.e. have no control over) the process which creates it. Air and water pollution are both examples of costs which are involuntarily borne by individuals outside the production process. Likewise, industrial and hazardous waste facilities may impose external costs on the host communities in the form of unpleasant noise, foul odors, increased traffic, or greater health risk.[1]

The crux of environmental justice concerns is that particular communities (chiefly those composed of people of color and the poor) have been forced to bear disproportionately the external costs of industrial processes. It follows, then, that one way of achieving environmental equity is to ensure that these costs are borne proportionately by all who reap the benefits of these processes. Policymakers have essentially three options for accomplishing this: eliminate all external costs of industrial processes; allocate the external costs evenly through the political system; or fairly compensate the individuals who bear these costs.

## Option one: Waste elimination—The "BANANA" principle

Many environmental justice advocates appear to desire above all else the complete elimination of pollution, so that *no* community has to bear the external costs of industrial processes. . . .

Clearly, the real cry of these environmental justice advocates goes beyond the familiar "NIMBY," or "not in my backyard." These activists are instead crying "BANANA"—"build absolutely nothing anywhere near anything" or, as one activist insisted "NOPE"—"not on planet earth."[2] Eliminating pollution would, of course, eradicate the problem of disproportionately distributed pollution, which is at the heart of the environmental justice issue. However, a moment of reflection on the BANANA principle, or a policy of complete waste elimination, reveals that such a policy is ultimately not feasible. Manufacturers simply cannot reduce pollution indefinitely without eliminating many valuable products and processes that Americans take for granted. In most cases, phasing out particular products is much more costly to society than accepting and treating the pollution required to create those products.

Consider, for example, pesticide use. In congressional testimony on environmental justice, activist Pat Bryant demanded action "at all levels" to stop the use of pesticides.[3] Certainly, Mr. Bryant was correct in asserting that high dosages of many pesticides may be harmful. But when *properly* used, chemical pesticides produce *net* social benefits in the form of higher per-acre crop yields and lower food prices. Eliminating pesticides would impose costs on society far greater than the costs the substances themselves impose.[4] Clearly, total pollution elimination is not an optimal solution.

Pollution reduction likewise has obvious limits.[5] As pollution is reduced further and further, the incremental cost of reducing each unit of pollution tends to rise and the incremental benefit associated with each unit of reduction falls. The optimal level of pollution reduction occurs at the point at which the incremental *cost* of abating an additional unit of pollution equals the incremental *benefit* of such abatement. Eliminating units of pollution beyond this point imposes costs on society greater than the costs incurred by the additional units of pollution.[6]

Later sections of this viewpoint suggest ways to encourage manufacturers to reduce pollution to the optimal level. It is clear, however, that a policy of preventing all pollution, while rhetorically effective, is neither socially optimal nor practicable.

## Option two: Allocate external costs politically

Because some pollution is inevitable in modern society, policymakers may decide that the best way to ensure environmental justice is to have the government determine which communities must host undesirable facilities. Of course, a purely political solution in which those in power simply decide where polluting and waste facilities should be located is probably not in the best interest of minorities and the economically disadvantaged, as these groups are typically underrepresented in the government. Most of those who advocate a political solution to environmental inequity argue instead for the establishment of nebulous legal and regulatory mechanisms that would force those in power to allocate pollution "fairly."

---

*Proposals to prohibit . . . polluting facilities from locating in minority and low-income communities deny those areas the economic benefits associated with hosting industrial waste plants.*

---

Unfortunately, it is difficult to pinpoint exactly what those legal and regulatory mechanisms are. For the most part, environmental justice advocates have refrained from proposing concrete political remedies for environmental inequities. While activists often suggest creating various offices, councils, and task forces, they rarely detail how these entities should influence the pollution allocation process. Though they advocate increased community involvement in siting decisions, they have yet to propose specific policies delineating how public participation is to be improved. Instead, environmental justice advocates have primarily sought to advance general concepts of equality, not wishing to endanger their coalition by specifying the precise methods of achieving "justice," "equity," and "fairness."

The few legal and regulatory mechanisms that have been suggested to remedy disparity in the allocation of pollution essentially boil down to two devices: 1) regulations which would directly limit or prohibit future industrial siting in minority and disadvantaged communities; and 2) penalties against presently active polluting and waste facilities that disproportionately impact minorities. The threat of such penalties, of course, would motivate facility owners to relocate or site future developments in nonminority neighborhoods.

*Siting Prohibitions.* Several proposals to prohibit siting in particular communities have recently been introduced in Congress. As expected, the bills have garnered significant support from environmental justice proponents. The Environmental Equal Rights Act of 1993 (H.R. 1924), introduced by Representative Cardiss Collins (D-Ill), would allow citizens to challenge and prohibit the construction of waste facilities in "environmentally disadvantaged communities." By definition, an environmentally disadvantaged community contains a higher than average percentage of low-income or minority residents and already hosts at least one waste facility, Superfund site, or facility which releases toxics. Any citizen of the state in which the facility has been proposed for siting may introduce a challenge; the challenger need not reside in the affected community.[7]

Under the Collins bill, a challenge would be granted and the proposed facility's construction and operating permits denied unless the facility proponent demonstrated that there is no alternative location in the state that poses fewer risks and that the proposed facility will neither release contaminants nor increase the impact of present contaminants.[8] Even if every resident of the potential host community desired that the facility be constructed and the sole challenger lived on the opposite end of the state, construction would be forbidden as long as the challenger demonstrated that the proposed community was in fact an environmentally disadvantaged community and that alternative locations were available.

A bill introduced in 1992 by then Senator Albert Gore (D-Tenn.) similarly sought to prohibit industrial siting in particular communities. Gore's bill, the Environmental Justice Act of 1992, called for a comprehensive survey of every county in the nation in an attempt to rank the 100 counties most severely contaminated by toxic chemical releases. The bill then provided for a moratorium on new pollution sources in those counties.[9]

A similar legislative proposal, the Environmental Justice Act of 1993 (H.R. 2105), was introduced in the 103rd Congress. The present bill differed from its predecessor by prohibiting new industrial activity only in those areas determined to receive toxic discharges in quantities found to adversely impact human health.[10]

Grassroots activists are joining legislators in calling for prohibitions on new industry in certain communities. In congressional testimony, Hazel Johnson of Chicago's People for Community Recovery called upon lawmakers to "place a moratorium on landfills and incinerators in residential areas."[11] Similarly, Pat Bryant, representing the Gulf Coast Tenants Association, called for "the Congress, state legislature, and local government[s] to legislate . . . an immediate moratorium on the siting of all hazardous waste facilities . . . and the placing of polluting and nuclear industries in the South."[12]

---

*Encouraging those who benefit from a facility to provide compensation to host communities . . . achieves a fairer distribution of environmental burdens and benefits.*

---

On the regulatory front, EPA is already making attempts to incorporate racial and socioeconomic considerations into permitting and siting programs. EPA Administrator Carol Browner recently vowed to "weave environmental justice concerns throughout all aspects of EPA policy and decision making."[13] According to Clarice Gaylord, director of the Agency's Office of Environmental Equity, "EPA offices are reevaluating how the siting and permitting process is used to determine where hazardous and solid waste facilities are placed." She insists, "Concerted efforts are being taken to work with state and local governments to incorporate socioeconomic factors into these decisions."[14]

The legislative proposals and the suggestions of grassroots activists are clear—the government must actively take steps to prohibit the siting of locally undesirable facilities in minority and low-income neighborhoods. EPA's initiatives are a bit more ambiguous. It is not immediately obvious how the agency will "weave environmental justice concerns" throughout all aspects of its decision making. Specifics aside, any reevaluation of siting and permitting processes to "incorporate socioeconomic factors" will likely have the effect of prohibiting the construction or operation of polluting and waste facilities in minority and low-income communities.

*Penalties for Disproportionate Impact.* The second method of politically allocating pollution does not directly prohibit or limit siting in minority and disadvantaged neighborhoods but instead *strongly discourages* the construction of polluting and waste facilities in such areas.

At the urging of environmental justice advocates, EPA recently opened investigations of environmental officials in Mississippi and Louisiana for allegedly violating Title VI of the 1964 Civil Rights Act. Under Title VI, which bans discrimination by federally funded programs, plaintiffs may prove discrimination by demonstrating that a federal program (e.g., a siting or permitting program) disproportionately impacts minorities. Plaintiffs need not establish that there was any intent to discriminate.[15]

While EPA's decision to open investigations under Title VI was somewhat controversial, Senator Paul Wellstone (D-Minn.) recently introduced legislation which would clear up any controversy surrounding the law's use. Explicitly applying Title VI to environmental agencies, Wellstone's bill, The Public Health Equity Act of 1994, would guarantee that discrimination judgments against siting and permitting agencies could be based solely upon a demonstration of disparate impact. There would no longer be any question as to whether plaintiffs must prove discriminatory intent. In Wellstone's words, his bill "mak[es] sure that government and the courts know [Title VI] applies" to environmental permitting agencies.

By merely demonstrating that differences in exposure exist, Title VI enables the government to deny companies needed building and operating permits and to withhold federal money destined for offending states. The threat of discrimination suits discourages government officials from permitting and facility owners from operating industrial plants in communities where such suits are likely to occur. Title VI effectively encourages facility owners to build away from poor and minority neighborhoods.

*Difficulties with the Proposed Political Solutions.* Both of the proposed political solutions to environmental inequity increase government control over the siting and permitting of locally undesirable facilities. The idea, of course, is that if the government has more influence in deciding where polluting and waste facilities operate, it can better assure that their negative externalities are fairly distributed.

---

*Inflexible siting and permitting policies which work to deny some individuals the opportunity to . . . substantially better themselves economically are patently paternalistic and ultimately unjust.*

---

Unfortunately, eliminating environmental inequity is not likely to be quite so simple. Prohibitions on siting (or disincentives to site) in minority and low-income neighborhoods are likely to economically harm the residents of those neighborhoods. Essentially, proposals to prohibit, limit, or discourage polluting facilities from locating in minority and low-income communities deny those areas the economic benefits associated with hosting industrial and waste plants. In many cases, these benefits far outweigh the cost of hosting such facilities. Affected communities should, therefore, be allowed to make trade-offs and decide for themselves whether or not to accept approved industrial activities. Policies which arbitrarily prohibit or discourage facility owners from siting in minority and low-income neighborhoods effectively preclude residents from deciding to accept comparatively small risks and inconveniences in exchange for substantial economic benefits.

Poor African-Americans in Brooksville, Mississippi, fully understand the downside of discouraging the construction of industrial and waste facilities in poor and minority communities. Because Brooksville rests upon a layer of impermeable chalk that would enclose waste and prevent seepage, Federated Technologies Industries of Mississippi (FTI) proposed to construct an incinerator and waste landfill in the town. While a local environmental group (Protect the Environment of Noxubee) and a group of middle-class black educators and ministers (African Americans for Environmental Justice) opposed toxic dumping in Brooksville and decried FTI's decision to site in the town as environmental racism, the local chapter of the National Association for the Advancement of Colored People (NAACP) supported construction of the facility.[16]

Instrumental in the local NAACP's decision to support FTI were the economic benefits the company promised the community. In addition to normal tax payments, FTI agreed to pay $250,000 every year into the county's general revenue fund. An additional $50,000 a year would be paid to the county for roadway construction and maintenance. Moreover, FTI agreed to build a civic center for the community, to finance a research center (to be a part of Mississippi State University), and to allot between 70 and 80 percent of the proposed facility's jobs to local residents.[17]

A group of local business owners also opposed construction of the dump in Brooksville. Their opposition may have stemmed from the fact that FTI guaranteed starting wages of between $7 and $8 and hour. Most of the factories and other businesses in Brooksville pay employees minimum wage or only slightly above.[18] Indeed, the local NAACP argued that many of those opposing the dump were trying to prevent a new employer from altering the area's low wage scale, thus keeping poor blacks "socially and economically oppressed."[19]

In late November 1993, FTI scrapped plans to build in Brooksville. The company is presently seeking permission to coordinate with another waste management company to construct a hazardous waste treatment center in Shuqualak, a town 18 miles south of Brooksville.

The residents of Brooksville, Mississippi, missed their chance to reap the economic benefits of hosting a waste treatment facility. Other economically disadvantaged communities have been more successful at working out lucrative partnerships with waste and industrial facilities. Consider the controversial Emelle landfill in Sumter County, Alabama. While often identified as an instance of discriminatory siting,[20] Emelle was actually sited in Sumter County because of the area's sparse population, arid climate, and location atop the "Selma chalk formation"—700 feet of dense, natural chalk. These factors, along with millions of dollars of State-of-the-art technology, make Emelle one of the world's safest landfills.[21]

Furthermore, the landfill provides over 400 jobs (60 percent of which are held by county residents), a $10 million annual payroll, and a guaranteed $4.2 million in annual tax revenue. This money has enabled the community to build a fire station and town hall, improve schools, upgrade the health-care delivery system, and begin reversing the rates of illiteracy and infant mortality.[22]

Black officials in Sumter County are apparently quite happy hosting the landfill. The all-black county commission has opposed state proposals that would have reduced the amount of waste the Emelle landfill accepts. "Financially, the landfill's been positive, very positive for the county," states Robert Smith, a black elementary school principal who now chairs the county commission.[23]

Clearly, it is possible for potential host communities to work out profitable agreements with polluting and waste facilities. To the extent that current environmental standards ensure minimal exposure risks, the primary costs associated with hosting a polluting or waste facility are "inconveniences" (i.e., odors, increased traffic, unpleasant noise, etc.). Community residents might find it in their best interest to endure these nuisances and minimal health risks in exchange for substantial economic benefits. However, policies which automatically prohibit or discourage facility owners from building in disadvantaged neighborhoods effectively eliminate opportunities for poor and minority communities to negotiate mutually beneficial arrangements with developers. By denying much-needed economic opportunities, such policies exacerbate the social ills which already plague many minority and low-income neighborhoods.

A second difficulty with political solutions to the environmental justice problem is that such policies are unlikely to be effective in the long run. Suggestions to remedy environmental inequity by prohibiting, limiting, or discouraging the construction of polluting and waste facilities in disadvantaged neighborhoods assume that "unfair" siting is the primary cause of disproportionate environmental impacts. Given this premise, it might seem that the best way to eliminate disparity is to reform siting and permitting procedures. The current research, however, fails to establish that environmental inequity results primarily from discriminatory siting practices.

The studies indicating the existence of racial disparities in pollution exposure fail to consider demographic conditions when local waste facilities were sited as well as alternate or additional explanations for higher concentrations of minority and low-income citizens near the plants. It is quite possible that polluting and waste facilities were originally sited "fairly," and that subsequent events led to present environmental inequities. To the extent that factors other than the siting and permitting processes caused disproportionate pollution exposure, policies which seek to alleviate disparity by dictating where facilities may locate are likely to be ineffective.

Recent research by New York University law professor Vicki Been indicates that siting and permitting procedures may not be the primary cause of disproportionately distributed pollution. Expanding University of California, Riverside, sociology professor Robert Bullard's analysis of environmental racism in the Houston area, Professor Been found that the dynamics of the housing market play a significant role in creating environmental inequities.[24, 25] . . .

After an industrial or waste facility moves into a neighborhood, the surrounding area is commonly perceived to be less desirable, and real estate prices fall. Indeed, an environmental justice study conducted by the University of Massachusetts, Amherst, found that the average value of homes in census tracts with TSDFs [waste treatment, storage, and disposal facilities] was approximately $11,000 less than the value of homes in other census tracts ($47,000 vs. $58,000).[26] Over time, the attractiveness of cheap housing will likely render many host communities low-income. A racially skewed income distribution, some degree of housing discrimination, and people's tendency to locate near others who are "like themselves" often cause these areas to have a larger share of non-white residents.[27]

To the extent that falling housing prices lead to minorities and the poor to "move to the nuisance," policies which focus on regulating where polluting and waste facilities may locate are unlikely to effectively eliminate environmental inequities. A better long-term solution would focus on providing compensating benefits to those who live near undesirable facilities, so that, on balance, the surrounding property is not rendered less desirable. Such compensating benefits would help eliminate the "white flight" that underlies many cases of alleged environmental racism.

Finally, even if increased siting restrictions were able to achieve a more racially balanced distribution of polluting and waste facilities, such policies would still not ensure environmental *justice*. In essence, the environmental justice issue rests upon two concerns: (1) that a few individuals (i.e., the residents of the community hosting a polluting or waste facility) are forced to bear the external costs of industrial processes from which the public at large receives benefits, *and* (2) that a disproportionate percentage of these individuals are minority or low-income citizens. Political solutions that simply inject racial and socioeconomic considerations into siting and permitting procedures address the latter concern, but not the former. These proposals seek to guarantee that the few individuals who *are* adversely affected are not minority or poor residents. The measures, however, do nothing to alleviate the first concern—the very fact that a few citizens must disproportionately bear the costs of processes that benefit everyone. In order to genuinely achieve environmental justice, policymakers should address this fundamental concern.

## Option three: Compensate individuals who bear external costs

A third possible solution to the environmental justice problem attempts to eliminate the primary environmental injustice by "diffusing" the concentrated external costs associated with a polluting or waste facility and compensating those individuals disproportionately impacted by the facility. There are primarily two methods of accomplishing both cost-diffusion and residential compensation. If the beneficiaries of a facility are somewhat well-defined (e.g., the residents of a multi-county region which shares a waste disposal facility), the government may use tax revenue from those citizens to compensate the host community. Alternatively, the undesirable facility could directly compensate local residents, reflecting the cost of doing so in the prices charged to those who utilize the facility's services. Under both schemes, the external costs of the facility are dispersed so that all who share its benefits also bear a portion of its costs. The fundamental difference between the two scenarios is that, in the former case, beneficiaries bear these costs wearing their taxpayer hat, while in the latter, they do so as consumers.

Economists refer to the procedure embodied in the second scheme as the "internalization" of external costs. Under such an approach, facility owners view the adverse local impact of their plant as part of their operating costs and charge prices sufficiently high to cover these costs—using the added revenue to compensate local residents.[28] As a result, pollution costs are no longer borne solely by those "outside" of the production process, but are, instead, equitably dispersed among those utilizing the facility's services. Due to offsetting benefits, residents of the host communities are, on balance, no worse off than they would be without the facilities.

The specific nature of these "offsetting benefits" may vary and should remain in the purview of the potential host community and the prospective developer. Some possible forms of compensation include direct payments to affected landowners, "host fees" which are paid into a community's general revenue fund and may be used to finance a variety of public projects or to lower property taxes, grants for improving local health-care delivery and education, and the provision of parks and other recreational amenities.

The compensation package offered Brooksville, Mississippi, for example, included direct payments to the community's general revenue fund, financing for roadway construction and maintenance, the establishment of various civic and research centers, and an agreement to provide the community with significant employment opportunities. In a less elaborate compensation agreement, Modern Landfill Inc. offered each citizen of Lewiston, New York, $960 annually for a 20-year period for the right to expand a landfill.[29]

With respect to the environmental justice issue, compensating individuals for bearing external costs entails at least two significant advantages.[30] Most importantly, compensation approaches are "just." Encouraging those who benefit from a facility to provide compensation to host communities alleviates the fundamental injustice in the status quo and achieves a fairer distribution of environmental burdens and benefits. Unlike the proposed political remedies for environmental inequities, which merely attempt to alter the socioeconomic and racial makeup of adversely affected communities, compensation assures that *no community* (regardless of race and income status) bears more than its fair share of environmental costs.

Of course, many may argue that it is immoral to "pay" individuals to expose themselves to health risks. These critics, however, should keep in mind the regulatory environment in which compensation agreements are negotiated. Present environmental standards are designed to guarantee a base level of environmental protection in which the exposure risks associated with polluting and waste facilities are quite minor. For example, the risk of developing cancer from living at the fence line of a properly constructed solid waste landfill is estimated to be one in a million. To put this in perspective, that's 30 times greater than the chance of being struck by lightning.

While many environmental justice advocates recite anecdotes of health problems in communities adjacent to licensed facilities and claim that present regulations are inadequate, they can produce no scientific data tying these alleged health problems to pollution exposure. However, should such a relationship be established, the appropriate policy response would be to raise the inadequate environmental standards, not to prevent individuals and facility owners from negotiating compensation agreements.[31] As long as environmental regulations guarantee minimal risk, there should be no moral difficulties with compensating individuals for voluntarily accepting the nuisances associated with waste and polluting facilities.

In fact, agreeing to host an industrial facility in exchange for compensating benefits can many times *improve* a community's public health. Often, the physical ailments that seem to plague low-income communities in industrial areas stem from inadequate nutrition and health care. In such cases, the best way to alleviate health problems is to provide the community with economic opportunities and a better health-care system. While compensation agreements can be negotiated to include job opportunities and funding for improved health services, political solutions which force industrial facilities out of low-income and minority areas will only increase rates of unemployment and poverty—conditions *proven* to impose significant health risks.

A second key advantage of compensation approaches is that they are more likely to guarantee a socially optimal level of pollution. As discussed earlier, society cannot indefinitely reduce pollution without eventually incurring costs greater than the costs of the pollution itself. Since both extremes—complete pollution elimination and reckless polluting—are undesirable, society must attempt to determine the optimal level of pollution abatement. Doing so requires a clear understanding of the full costs and benefits associated with a proposed facility. By negotiating compensation arrangements, the developer and the host community illuminate social costs, which would otherwise remain unaccounted for. As such, compensation arrangements better enable decision makers to determine when and where to reduce pollution.

Consider, for example, the negotiations surrounding the siting of a hypothetical solid waste incinerator. Throughout the negotiating proceedings, the proposed host community gathers information concerning the local impact of the incinerator's operations. Using this information, it determines the minimum compensation required to host the facility. The developer must then decide whether to accept the community's compensation demands, implement additional pollution abatement devices so as to reduce the level of pollution exposure and the consequent compensation requirement, or focus on an alternative host site. In some instances, the external costs associated with a proposed facility may be so high as to make it unprofitable in any location. A compensation approach helps weed out such ill-conceived industrial projects.[32] In any case, negotiating compensation agreements illuminates the full costs and benefits of industrial activity and better enables society to make trade-offs between industrial expansion and environmental protection.

To the extent that environmental justice advocates want to strike a proper balance between pollution prevention and much-needed economic development, they should support a compensation approach. Increasingly, private developers are using negotiated compensation as a mechanism for diffusing local opposition. Nevertheless, a number of obstacles remain in the way of wide spread compensation agreements. While it is beyond the scope of this study to suggest specific legislative proposals, a brief examination of one state statute demonstrates how legislators can encourage the use of such agreements.

Wisconsin's landfill negotiation/arbitration statute was adopted in 1981 with the intent to not only make the siting of waste facilities more efficient, but also to accommodate the legitimate concerns of local residents and municipalities. The principal mechanism by which the legislation accomplishes both of these goals is the requirement that any developer wishing to site a landfill must first establish negotiations with the affected municipalities.[33] During these negotiations, any subject is open for discussion "except the need for the facility and any proposal that would make the [developer's] responsibilities less stringent than required by the Department of Natural Resources."[34] In principle, negotiations can continue until all of the parties' concerns are resolved. If a settlement has not been reached after a "reasonable period," however, one or both of the parties can request that the case be turned over to binding arbitration.

Thus far, the Wisconsin program has seemingly worked very well. Since the law took effect in 1982, only 3 of the 150 submitted permit applications have been arbitrated.[35] Officials with waste management organizations are apparently quite happy with the landfill arbitration/negotiation statute. According to Joe Suchechi, manager of government affairs for WMX Technologies, Inc., requiring compensation negotiations makes it "much easier" to site and expand waste facilities in Wisconsin than in other states, where developers and potential host communities are often polarized. By involving the local community and formalizing negotiation procedures, the Wisconsin law, states Suchechi, creates a "process that gets everyone to the right place."[36]

The virtue of the Wisconsin legislation as a model is that it includes several principles which are necessary for compensation agreements to be successful. First, the Wisconsin statute clearly specifies "the players of the game"—that is, who negotiates with whom. Both developers and potential host communities are required to establish negotiating committees, with the rules regarding these representatives explicitly set forth in the statute. Secondly, the legislation assures that these "players" will not only negotiate, but also that the results of their negotiations will be legally binding. The fulcrum of the legislation is its prohibition against constructing or operating a new facility without a "siting agreement," which records the conditions and compensation to be exacted by the community from the developer, any voluntary commitments of the developer, as well as the promises made by local government officials. Without such legally binding authority, the parties have fewer incentives to negotiate in good faith. Finally, the Wisconsin statute provides a "back-up plan"— a way to arbitrate siting decisions should negotiations fail or should one party refuse to cooperate. Each of these criteria is crucial if negotiated compensation agreements are to be successfully applied to environmental justice issues.

## Conclusion

In the flurry of activity surrounding the environmental justice issue, policymakers should not lose sight of two basic themes. First, despite a number of high-profile studies, the existing research does not substantiate environmental justice advocates' claims of discriminatory siting. While the issue of environmental racism may be persuasive in theory, it is requisite upon the proponents of government intervention to demonstrate, using sound statistical data, both that environmental inequities really exist as well as the specific factors which generate them. Thus far, neither has occurred. Therefore, it is premature to enact regulatory "solutions."

Secondly, none of the proposed political remedies for environmental racism address the primary injustice known to exist in the status quo: the fact that a few individuals are forced to bear the external costs of industrial processes from which the public at large receives benefits. A compensation approach, in which those who share the benefits of a locally undesirable facility provide offsetting benefits to those who bear the costs of hosting the plant, directly confronts this issue. By providing affected individuals a place at the negotiating table, compensation schemes empower them to have a say in how pollution is allocated and ensure that *all* communities (regardless of their racial or socioeconomic makeup) fairly share the advantages of socially beneficial industries.

Justice ultimately amounts to "treating equals equally." Justice thus involves respecting the autonomy and individual dignity of each citizen. Inflexible siting and permitting policies which work to deny some individuals the opportunity to accept small risks and inconveniences in order to substantially better themselves economically are patently paternalistic and ultimately unjust. Justice is better served when each community is granted both the right to be free from uncompensated external costs and the freedom to negotiate appropriate compensation.

## *Notes*

1. For further discussion of pollution as a negative externality, see Tom Tietenberg, *Environmental and Natural Resource Economics*, Third Ed., (New York: HarperCollins, 1992), pp. 51-59.

2. William K. Reilly, "The Green Thumb of Capitalism," 54 *Policy Review* 16 (1990).

3. Pat Bryant representing the Gulf Coast Tenants Association, Testimony submitted to the Subcommittee on Civil and Constitutional Rights of the Committee on the Judiciary of the U.S. House of Representatives, March 3, 1993, p.5.

4. It should also be noted that, with respect to pesticides, these higher costs are borne disproportionately by minorities and the poor, who spend a greater percentage of their income on basic food items.

5. See James Lis with Kenneth Chilton, *The Limits of Pollution Prevention*, Contemporary Issues Series 52, (St. Louis: Center for the Study of American Business, May 1992).

6. Consider, for example, the increasing incremental costs and decreasing incremental benefits of cleaning up the industrial effluent of paper factories. Between 1970 and 1978, it cost the pulp and paper industry $3 billion to achieve a 95 percent reduction in its water effluents. To reach a 98 percent reduction level by 1984—a goal proposed by EPA at that time— the industry would have had to spend an additional $4.8 billion. See Murray L. Weidenbaum, *Business, Government, and the Public*, Sec. Ed., (Englewood Cliffs, N.J.: Prentice Hall, Inc., 1981), p.354.

7. *Congressional Record*, House of Representatives, April 30, 1993, p. E1106.

8. Ibid.

9. *Congressional Record*, Senate, June 3, 1993, p. S7489.

10. H.R. 2105, 103d Congress, First Session (1993).

11. Hazel Johnson representing People for Community Development, testimony before the Subcommittee on Civil and Constitutional Rights of the Committee on the Judiciary of the U.S. House of Representatives, March 3, 1993, p.4.

12. Pat Bryant congressional testimony, March 3, 1993, p.3.

13. Stephen C. Jones, "EPA Targets Environmental Racism," *National Law Journal*, August 9, 1993, p.28.

14. Clarice Gaylord representing the Office of Environmental Equity of the U.S. Environmental Protection Agency, testimony before the Subcommittee on Civil and Constitution Rights of the Committee on the Judiciary of the U.S. House of Representatives, March 3, 1993, p.5.

15. For a detailed discussion of the use of Title VI see Richard J. Lazarus, "Pursuing 'Environmental Justice:' The Distributional Effects of Environmental Protection," *Northwestern University Law Review*, vol. 87, no. 3, pp. 787-857.

16. Keith Schneider, "Plan for Toxic Dump Pits Blacks Against Blacks," the *New York Times*, December 13, 1993, p. A7.

17. Telephone conversation with Richard Brooks, alderman of Brooksville and president of the local NAACP, December 14, 1993.

18. Ibid.

19. Schneider, p. A7.

20. See "A Place at the Table," *Sierra*, May/June 1993, p.52; and Robert Bullard, "The Threat of Environmental Racism," *Natural Resources and the Environment*, Winter 1993, p.25.

21. Charles McDermott representing Waste Management, Inc., testimony before the Subcommittee on Civil and Constitutional Rights of the Committee on the Judiciary of the U.S. House of Representatives, March 3, 1993, p.11.

22. Ibid., p.12 and Tom Arrandale, "When the Poor Cry NIMBY," *Governing*, September 1993, p. 40.

23. Arrandale, p.40.

24. Vicki Been, "Locally Undesirable Land Uses in Minority Neighborhoods: Disproportionate Siting or Market Dynamics," 103 *Yale Law Journal* 6, April 1994.

25. Robert Bullard, "Solid Waste Sites and the Black Houston Community," 53 *Social Inquiry* 273, 1983.

26. Douglas Anderton et al., "Hazardous Waste Facilities: 'Environmental Equity' Issues in Metropolitan Areas" (Amherst: Social and Demographic Research Institute, University of Massachusetts and Northeast Regional Environmental Public Health Center) Published in Evaluation Review, Vol. 18, No. 2, April 1994, Table 1.

27. For evidence of race differences in income distribution, see James P. Smith and Finis Welch, "Race Differences in Earnings: A Survey and New Evidence," in *Current Issues in Urban Economics*, eds. Peter Mieszkowski and Mahlon Straszheim, (Baltimore: Johns Hopkins University Press, 1979), pp. 40-73. For a discussion of discrimination in the housing market, see John M. Quigley, "Prejudice and Discrimination in the Urban Housing Market," also in *Current Issues in Urban Economics*, pp. 430-468. For evidence that individuals' decisions to relocate and their choice of neighborhoods is influenced by a desire to be near others who are "like me," see William M. Dobriner, *Class in Suburbia*, 1963, pp. 64-67.

28. Presumably, the facility would be the only one of its type in the area, so that higher prices would not motivate residents to stop using its services. This "inelastic demand" would ensure that increased revenue from higher prices would not be offset by a decrease in demand for the facility's services.

29. Herbert Inhaber, "Of LULUs, NIMBYs, and NIMTOOs," 107 *Public Interest* 52, 63 (1992).

30. Compensation approaches entail a third significant benefit which is less directly related to the environmental justice issue: increased efficiency in the siting process. Typically, local citizens oppose the construction or expansion of polluting or waste facilities because they expect that the plants will impose net costs upon them. By decreasing a host community's "expected net cost," facility proponents may diminish or eliminate local opposition to construction or expansion. Compensation agreements reduce the net cost each neighbor expects to suffer should a facility be built and thereby diffuse local motivation to oppose proposed developments. In many cases, the cost of compensating hosts may be less than the cost of defending proposed projects. Increasingly, developers are voluntarily negotiating compensation agreements with host communities. See Inhaber, "Of LULUs . . ." and Michael O'Hare " 'Not on My Block You Don't': Facility Siting and the Strategic Importance of Compensation," 25 *Public Policy* 407 (1977).

31. Many environmental justice advocates, for example, insist that present environmental standards do not adequately protect human health because they fail to account for cumulative exposure risks in an area (i.e., they do not consider the other pollution sources in the community). If this is the case, regulators should raise the standards for new facilities in order to guarantee a base level of protection. Regulators should not directly prohibit new facilities, nor should they hinder compensation negotiations. The more stringent regulations necessary to guarantee a base level of health protection may motivate new pollution sources to locate elsewhere. However, new facilities may be able to meet the higher standards or to provide for increased pollution abatement at other local facilities in order to achieve the base level of health protection.

32. Some critics argue that compensation approaches allow communities to halt industrial development by raising their minimum compensation demands to a level that is too high for developers to pay. However, because potential host communities risk losing benefits if they require too much compensation, they have an incentive not to inflate their compensation demands.

33. Failure on the part of a developer to participate in negotiations will result in the denial of necessary licenses and operating permits. On the other hand, if local communities refuse to negotiate or negotiate in bad faith, a developer may petition the Waste Facility Siting Board to be relieved of the negotiation requirement and proceed with the project via traditional regulatory channels. See "Wisconsin's Landfill Negotiation/Arbitration Statute," Peter Ruud and Dean Werner, *Wisconsin Bar Bulletin*, November 1985, pp. 17-19, 64-65.

34. "Standard Notice," sent to municipalities by the state of Wisconsin, Waste Facility Siting Board.

35. Telephone conversation with Patti Cronin, Executive Director of State of Wisconsin Waste Facility Siting Board, March 2, 1994.

36. Telephone conversation with Joe Suchechi, manager of government affairs, WMX Technologies Inc., March 3, 1994.

# 8

# The Global Policies of the United States Are Environmentally Unjust

### John Bellamy Foster

*John Bellamy Foster, professor of sociology at the University of Oregon in Eugene, is a regular contributor to the* Monthly Review, *an independent socialist magazine, and author of* The Vulnerable Planet, *published by the Monthly Review Press.*

If the lives of Third World citizens are worth less economically than the lives of people in industrialized nations—based on their lower wages and shorter life spans—then "the logic of dumping a load of toxic waste in the lowest wage country is impeccable," to quote chief economist of the World Bank Lawrence Summers. The openly exploitative nature of this economic logic, especially issuing from the head of an institution charged with maintaining the global economy, is shocking—but it is also the guiding principle behind the 20 million tons of waste shipped from developed countries to the Third World each year. It is, moreover, a global dimension of the disproportionate distribution of environmental hazards within the United States, where minority communities bear the majority of these burdens. As the leader of the capitalist world, the United States is committed to maintaining environmental inequity, a position it demonstrated in 1992 at the Earth Summit in Brazil by opposing treaties protecting the environment. But in protecting its global profits the United States is only hastening the certain demise of the planet—an eventuality that capitalism cannot comprehend.

On December 12, 1991, Lawrence Summers, chief economist of the World Bank, sent a memorandum to some of his colleagues presenting views on the environment that are doubtless widespread among orthodox economists, reflecting as they do the logic of capital accumulation, but which are seldom offered up for public scrutiny, and then almost never by an economist of Summers' rank. This memo was later leaked to the British publication, *The Economist*, which published part of it on February 8, 1992, under the title "Let Them Eat Pollution." The published part of the memo is quoted in full below:

> Just between you and me, shouldn't the World Bank be encouraging *more* migration of the dirty industries to the LDCs [Less Developed Countries]? I can think of three reasons:
>
> (1) The measurement of the costs of health-impairing pollution depends on the foregone earnings from increased morbidity and mortality. From this point of view a given amount of health-impairing pollution should be done in the country with the lowest cost, which will be the country of the lowest wages. I think the economic logic behind dumping a load of toxic waste in the lowest-wage country is impeccable and we should face up to that.
>
> (2) The costs of pollution are likely to be non-linear as the initial increments of pollution will probably have very low cost. I've always thought that under-populated countries in Africa are vastly *under*polluted; their air quality is probably vastly inefficiently low [sic] compared to Los Angeles or Mexico City. Only the lamentable facts that so much pollution is generated by non-tradeable industries (transport, electrical generation) and that the unit transport costs of solid waste are so high prevent world-welfare-enhancing trade in air pollution and waste.
>
> (3) The demand for a clean environment for aesthetic and health reasons is likely to have very high income-elasticity. The concern over an agent that causes a one-in-a-million change in the odds of prostate cancer is obviously going to be much higher in a country where people survive to get prostate cancer than in a country where under-five mortality is 200 per thousand. Also, much of the concern over industrial atmospheric discharge is about visibility-impairing particulates. These discharges may have very little direct health impact. Clearly trade in goods that embody aesthetic pollution concerns could be welfare-enhancing. While production is mobile the consumption of pretty air is a non-tradeable.
>
> The problem with the arguments against all of these proposals for more pollution in LDCs (intrinsic rights to certain goods, moral rights, social concerns, lack of adequate markets, etc.) [is that they] could be turned around and used more or less effectively against every Bank proposal for liberalization.

The World Bank later told *The Economist* that in writing his memo Summers had intended to "provoke debate" among his Bank colleagues, while Summers himself said that he had not meant to advocate "the dumping of untreated toxic wastes near the homes of poor people." Few acquainted with orthodox economics, however, can doubt that the central arguments utilized in the memo were serious. In the view of *The Economist* itself (February 15, 1992), Summers' language was objectionable but "his economics was hard to answer."

## Restating the facts

Although its general meaning could not be clearer, this entire memo deserves to be summarized and restated in a way that will bring out some of the more subtle implications. First, the lives of individuals in the Third World, judged by "foregone earnings" from illness and death, are worth less—the same logic says frequently hundreds of times less—than those of individuals in the advanced capitalist countries where wages are often hundreds of times higher. The low wage periphery is therefore the proper place in which to dispose of globally produced toxic wastes if the overall economic value of human life is to be maximized worldwide. Second, Third World countries are "vastly *under*polluted" in the sense that their air pollution levels are "inefficiently low" when compared with highly polluted cities like Los Angeles and Mexico City (where schoolchildren had to be kept home for an entire month in 1989 because of the abysmal air quality). Third, a clean environment can be viewed as a luxury good pursued by rich countries with high life expectancies where higher aesthetic and health standards apply; worldwide costs of production would therefore fall if polluting industries were shifted from the center to the periphery of the world system. Hence, for all of these reasons the World Bank should encourage the migration of polluting industries and toxic wastes to the Third World. Social and humanitarian arguments against such world trade in waste, Summers concludes, can be disregarded since they are the same arguments that are used against all proposals for capitalist development.

It is important to understand that this policy perspective, with the utter contempt that it displays both for the world's poor and the world environment, is by no means an intellectual aberration. As the World Bank's chief economist Summers' role is to help create conditions conducive to world capital accumulation, particularly where the core of the capitalist world system is concerned. Neither the welfare of the majority of the population of the globe nor the ecological fate of the earth—nor even the fate of individual capitalists themselves—can be allowed to stand in the way of this single-minded goal.

Perhaps the most shocking part of the Summers memo is the openly exploitative attitude that it demonstrates toward the world's poor. And yet nothing is more characteristic of bourgeois economics. *The Economist*, which went on to defend Summers' general conclusions about the desirability of the migration of polluting industries to the Third World in subsequent commentaries, nonetheless dismissed Summers' specific references to the valuation of life as "crass," denying that such exploitative attitudes toward human life are likely to play an explicit role in government policy in free societies. "Few governments," *The Economist* stated in its February 15, 1992, issue, "would care to defend a policy based on differences in valuations among groups—arguing, for instance, that society values an extra year of life for a white-collar worker more highly than for a blue-collar worker. Yet this is the counterpart, within a rich country, of what Summers appeared to be suggesting for the Third World." The truth, however, as *The Economist* itself admitted at another point in the same article, is that governments constantly do make decisions—whether in regard to health, education, working conditions, housing, environment, etc.—that are "based on differences in valuations" among classes, whether or not they "care to defend" their policies in this way. Indeed, such differences in valuation, as anyone with the slightest knowledge of history and economics must realize, are at the very core of the capitalist economy and state.

## The U.S. example

To illustrate this we only need to turn to the United States. The OMB (Office of Management and Budget) under the Reagan administration endeavored to promote calculations of the dollar value of a human life based on "the wage premiums that workers require for accepting jobs with increased risk." On this basis a number of academic studies concluded that the value of a worker's life in the United States is between $500,000 and $2 million (far less than the annual salary of many corporate CEOs). The OMB then used these results to argue that some forms of pollution abatement were cost-effective, while others were not, in accordance with President Reagan's executive order No. 12291 that regulatory measures should "be chosen to maximize the net benefit to society."

"Some economists," Barry Commoner informs us,

> . . . have proposed that the value of a human life should be based on a person's earning power. It then turns out that a woman's life is worth much less than a man's, and that a black's life is worth much less than a white's. Translated into environmental terms, harm is regarded as small if the people at hazard are poor—an approach that could be used to justify locating heavily polluting operations in poor neighborhoods. This is, in fact, only too common a practice. A recent study shows, for example, that most toxic dumps are located near poor black and Hispanic communities.

In 1983 a study by the U.S. General Accounting Office determined that three out of the four off-site commercial hazardous waste landfills in the southern states were located in primarily black communities even though blacks represented only 20 percent of the population in the region.[1]

Summers' argument for dumping toxic wastes in the Third World is therefore nothing more than a call for the globalization of policies and practices which are already evident in the United States, and which have recently been unearthed in locations throughout the capitalist world. The developed countries ship millions of tons of waste to the Third World and Eastern Europe each year. In 1987 dioxin-laden industrial ash from Philadelphia was dumped in Guinea and Haiti. In 1988 4,000 tons of PCB-contaminated chemical waste from Italy was found in Nigeria, leaking from thousands of rusting and corroding drums, poisoning both soil and groundwater.[2] There can be few more blatant examples of the continuing dominance of imperialism over Third World affairs.

---

*Summers' argument for dumping toxic wastes in the Third World is therefore nothing more than a call for the globalization of policies . . . in the United States.*

---

This same frame of mind, which sees toxic pollution less as a problem to be overcome than one to be managed in accordance with the logic of the free market, is evident in the approach adopted by orthodox economists to issues as fateful as global warming. Writing in the May 30, 1992, issue of *The Economist*, Summers illustrates this perspective and the general attitude of the World Bank by stating that,

> The argument that a moral obligation to future generations demands special treatment of environmental investments is fatuous. We can help our descendants as much by improving infrastructure as by preserving rain forests . . . as much by enlarging our scientific knowledge as by reducing carbon dioxide in the air. . . . The reason

why some investments favored by environmentalists fail . . . a [rigorous cost-benefit] test is that their likely effect on living standards is not so great. . . . In the worst-case scenario of the most pessimistic estimates yet prepared (those of William Cline of the Institute for International Economics), global warming reduces growth over the next two centuries by less than 0.1 percent a year. More should be done: dealing with global warming would not halt economic growth either. But raising the specter of our impoverished grandchildren if we fail to address global environmental problems is demagoguery.

The problem with such arguments is that they are based on forms of economic calculation that consistently undervalue natural wealth and underestimate the dependence of the economy on ecological conditions. The rebuilding of infrastructure cannot be equated with preserving the world's tropical rainforests since the loss of the latter would be irrevocable and would mean the extinction of both a majority of the world's species and the world's greatest genetic library. The absurdity of William Cline's attempt to quantify the potential economic damages of "very long-term global warming" up through the year 2300—to which Summers refers—should be apparent to anyone who considers the obvious impossibility of applying economic values to the scale of climatic change anticipated. Thus the Cline estimates are based on a projected rise in global mean temperatures of 10° to 18° C (18° to 32° F) by the year 2300. The cost of this to the U.S. economy, Cline expects us to believe, will be long-term damages equal to 6 to 12 percent of GNP under the best assumptions, 20 percent under the worst.[3] All of this is nonsense, however, from an ecological standpoint, since a temperature rise of 4° C would create an earth that was warmer than at any time in the last 40 million years. In the midst of the last ice age the earth was only 5° C colder than it is today. Viewed from this standpoint the question of whether or not long-term damages would equal 6, 12 or 20 percent of GNP must give way to the more rational question of whether human civilization and life itself could persist in the face of such a drastic change in global temperatures.

## Defending development—at all costs

An even more alarming example of the same general argument was provided, again in the May 30, 1992, issue of *The Economist*, in a special report published in advance of the June 1992 Earth Summit in Rio. After examining estimates on the economic costs and benefits of averting global warming and the political obstacles to change under existing capitalist regimes, *The Economist* declares:

The chances that the climate treaty will significantly change the world's output of fossil fuels over the next century is extremely slender. Does this matter? If the figures . . . for the costs of damage likely to be done by climate change are accurate, then the honest answer is "no." It would be, of course, wise for countries to take the free lunches available to them . . . and to price their energy sensibly. It might be wise to go some way beyond that point, in the interests of buying insurance against nasty surprises. . . . Beyond that, adapting to climate change, when it happens, is undoubtedly the most rational course, for a number of reasons. Most countries will be richer then, and so better able to afford to build sea walls or develop drought resistant plants. Money that might now be spent on curbing carbon-dioxide output can be invested instead, either in

preventing more damaging environmental change (like rapid population growth, the most environmentally harmful trend of all) or
in productive assets that will generate future income to pay for
adaptation. Once climate change occurs, it will be clearer—as it
now is not—how much needs to be done, and what, and where.
Most of the decisions involved in adapting will be taken and paid
for by the private sector rather than (as with curbing greenhouse-
gas output) by government. Above all, adapting requires no international agreements.[4]

The answer then is "let them build sea walls or develop drought resistant plants." And this in response to "very probable" rises in global
mean temperature of 1.5° to 5.0° C (2.7° to 9° F) over the next century if
"business as usual" continues, a prospect that scientists all over the world
regard as potentially catastrophic for the entire planet![5] The threat of heat
waves, droughts, floods, and famines suggests the likelihood of incalcula-
ble losses in lives, species, ecosystems, and cultures. Nevertheless, for *The
Economist* the adaptation of the capital accumulation process and thus
world civilization to irreversible global warming once it has taken place
and many of its worst effects are evident is easy to contemplate, while any
attempt to head off disaster—however defensible in social, moral, and
ecological terms—besides being difficult to institute under present-day
capitalist regimes—would interfere with the dominance of capital and
must therefore be unthinkable.

The wait and see attitude promoted by *The Economist* was of course the
general stance adopted by the United States (and to a lesser extent Britain)
at the Earth Summit. Through its actions in watering down the climate
treaty, refusing to sign the biological diversity treaty, and hindering initiatives on weapons of mass destruction and nuclear waste, the United
States signaled in no uncertain terms that it was prepared to take on the
task of opposing radical forces within the global environmental movement, adding this to its larger role as the leading defender of the capitalist world. According to the U.S. government's position, the concept of
"sustainable development" means first and foremost that any environmental goals that can be interpreted as interfering with development must
be blocked. Thus in his defense of U.S. intransigence on global environmental issues at the Earth Summit in June 1992 George Bush explained, "I
think it is important that we take both those words—environment and development—equally seriously. And we do." No environmental action
could therefore be taken, Bush declared, that would jeopardize U.S. economic interests. "I am determined to protect the environment. I am also
determined to protect the American taxpayer. The day of the open check-
book is over . . . environmental protection and a growing economy are inseparable." In what was intended not only as a re-election ploy but also a
declaration of U.S. priorities where questions of environmental costs and
controls were concerned, Bush declared, "For the past half century the
United States has been the great engine of global economic growth, and
it's going to stay that way." (*Guardian* [London], June 13, 1992)

## Capitalism against the world

The consequences of such short-sighted attention to economic growth
and profit before all else are of course enormous, since they call into question the survivability of the entire world. It is an inescapable fact that human history is at a turning point, the result of a fundamental change in

the relationship between human beings and the environment. The scale at which people transform energy and materials has now reached a level that rivals elemental natural processes. Human society is adding carbon to the atmosphere at a level that is equal to about 7 percent of the natural carbon exchange of atmosphere and oceans. The carbon dioxide content of the atmosphere as a result has grown by a quarter in the last 200 years, with more than half of this increase since 1950. Human beings now use (take or transform) 25 percent of the plant mass fixed by photosynthesis over the entire earth, land and sea, and 40 percent of the photosynthetic product on land. Largely as a result of synthetic fertilizers, humanity fixes about as much nitrogen in the environment as does nature. With human activities now rivaling nature in scale, actions that in the past merely produced local environmental crises now have global implications. Moreover, environmental effects that once seemed simple and trivial, such as increases in carbon dioxide emissions, have now suddenly become threats to the stability of the fundamental ecological cycles of the planet. Destruction of the ozone layer, the greenhouse effect, annihilation of ancient and tropical forests, species extinction, reductions in genetic diversity, production of toxic and radioactive wastes, contamination of water resources, soil depletion, depletion of essential raw materials, desertification, the growth of world population spurred by rising poverty—all represent ominous trends the full impact of which, singly or in combination, is scarcely to be imagined at present. "With the appearance of a continent-sized hole in the Earth's protective ozone layer and the threat of global warming," Barry Commoner has written, "even droughts, floods, and heat waves may become unwitting acts of man."[6]

---

*The developed countries ship millions of tons of waste to the Third World and Eastern Europe each year.*

---

The sustainability of both human civilization and global life processes depends not on the mere slowing down of these dire trends, but on their *reversal*.[7] Nothing in the history of capitalism, however, suggests that the system will be up to such a task. On the contrary there is every indication that the system, left to its own devices, will gravitate toward the "let them eat pollution" stance so clearly enunciated by the chief economist of the World Bank.

Fortunately for the world, however, capitalism has never been allowed to develop for long entirely in accordance with its own logic. Opposition forces always emerge—whether in the form of working class struggles for social betterment or conservation movements dedicated to overcoming environmental depredations—that force the system to moderate its worst tendencies. And to some extent the ensuing reforms can result in lasting, beneficial constraints on the market. What the capitalist class cannot accept, however, are changes that will likely result in the destruction of the system itself. Long before reform movements threaten the accumulation process as a whole, therefore, counterforces are set in motion by the ruling interests, and the necessary elemental changes are headed off.

And there's the rub. Where radical change is called for little is accomplished within the system and the underlying crisis intensifies over time. Today this is particularly evident in the ecological realm. For the nature of the global environmental crisis is such that the fate of the entire planet and social and ecological issues of enormous complexity are involved, all traceable to the forms of production now prevalent. It is impossible to prevent the world's environmental crisis from getting progressively worse unless root problems of production, distribution, technology, and growth are dealt with on a global scale. And the more that such questions are raised, the more it becomes evident that capitalism is unsustainable—ecologically, economically, politically, and morally—and must be superseded.

## Notes

1. Barry Commoner, *Making Peace with the Planet* (New York: The New Press, 1992), pp. 64-66; Robert Bullard, "The Politics of Race and Pollution: An Interview with Robert Bullard," *Multinational Monitor* (vol. 13, no. 6. June 1992), pp. 21-22.

2. Bill Weinberg, *War on the Land* (London: Zed Books, 1991), pp. 37-39; Edward Goldsmith, et al., *The Imperilled Planet* (Cambridge, Mass.: MIT Press, 1990), p. 147; Center for Investigative Reporting and Bill Moyers, *Global Dumping Ground* (Cambridge: The Lutterworth Press, 1991), pp. 1-2, 12; Third World Network, *Toxic Terror* (Penang, Malaysia: Third World Network, 1989), pp. 8-25.

3. William R. Cline, *The Economics of Global Warming* (Washington, D.C.: Institute for International Economics, 1992), pp. 4-6, 55-58, 130-33, 300.

4. See also Frances Cairncross, *Costing the Earth* (London: Economist Books, 1991), pp. 30-31, 130-33.

5. National Academy of Sciences, *One Earth, One Future* (Washington, D.C.: National Academy Press, 1990), pp. 67-71; Helen Caldicott, *If You Love This Planet* (New York: W. W. Norton, 1992), p. 24; Mostafa K. Tolba, *Saving Our Planet* (New York: Chapman and Hall, 1992), pp. 27-28; Intergovernmental Panel on Climate Change, *Climate Change* (New York: Cambridge University Press, 1990), p. xxii.

6. IPCC, *Climate Change*, p. xvi; Donella Meadows, et al., *Beyond the Limits* (London: Earthscan, 1992), pp. 65-66; Jim MacNeill, et al., *Beyond Interdependence* (New York Oxford University Press, 1991), pp. 8-9; Paul R. Ehrlich and Anne H. Ehrlich, *Healing the Planet* (New York: Addison-Wesley, 1991), pp. 26-27; Peter M. Vitousek, et al., "Human Appropriation of the Products of Photosynthesis," *Bioscience* (vol. 36, no. 6, June 1986), pp. 368-73; Commoner, p. 3.

7. Paul M. Sweezy, "Capitalism and the Environment," *Monthly Review* (vol. 41, no. 2, June 1989), p. 6; Meadows, *Beyond the Limits*, p. xv.

# 9

# Halting the Trade in Recyclable Wastes Will Hurt Developing Countries

## Harvey Alter

*Harvey Alter is manager of the Resources Policy Department at the United States Chamber of Commerce in Washington, D.C., and serves on two U.S. Environmental Protection Agency advisory committees on hazardous waste. He is also adjunct professor at the University College graduate School of Management and Technology, University of Maryland.*

After a number of blatant cases of hazardous waste dumping on developing countries, several nations met under the auspices of the United Nations in 1989 and drafted the Basel Convention on the Control of Transboundary Movements of Hazardous Wastes and Their Disposal. But in trying to protect developing countries from receiving undesirable garbage, the Basel Convention's poorly articulated "hazardous waste" definitions effectively prevent these countries from obtaining the recyclable portion of the scrap metal, paper, and other secondary raw materials they need to produce value-added commodities (the value being added by processing the raw materials) for resale. In a similar way, a March 1994 ban on the trade in wastes for recycling between developed and developing countries will further deprive the latter of jobs and foreign exchange, while failing to curtail the sizeable and potentially harmful trade in hazardous waste between developing countries. The ban will also severely limit the transfer from developed to developing countries of technology to assure environmentally sound waste management practices. The net effect of the convention's definitional problems and the waste trade ban will be the deepening poverty of the developing nations, a poverty that will exacerbate the environmental problems these actions were trying to alleviate.

People were shocked in the 1980s by news stories of shipments of municipal and industrial wastes from the United States and Europe going to developing countries. One ship sailed from port to port, unable to unload

Harvey Alter, "Controlling International Trade in Wastes," August 1994. Written expressly for inclusion in the present volume.

its cargo of waste, sailing the seas like the mythical Flying Dutchman [the *Mobro 4000*, a garbage barge that in 1987 traveled for six months, docking at several harbors, before returning its load to its origin in New York].

Some of the reports at that time were close to rumor; others received detailed coverage and attention. A few developing countries may have wanted to earn foreign exchange from waste management services, but any such opportunities were lost. Just a few shipments became world symbols of egregious disregard for people and the environment.

In response, during 1989 under the leadership of the United Nations Environment Programme, countries concluded an international agreement, the *Basel Convention on the Control of Transboundary Movements of Hazardous Wastes and Their Disposal*. Through the first half of 1994, 68 countries had ratified the Convention, which means they have domestic legislation in place to enforce their duties and responsibilities under the agreement. By that time, an additional 38 countries had signed the Convention, which is a statement of intent to ratify or become a "Party."[1]

The Basel Convention requires that when someone in one country wants to ship hazardous waste to another, he or she must notify the government of the receiving country and obtain written permission. If a country does not want to import a waste, it can deny permission for any reason and prevent the importation.

There are still occasional news reports of mis-shipments and claims of another country's waste's affecting the health and well-being of workers in an importing country. Graphic and heart-rending photographs have been published of poor people painstakingly handling plastics garbage or living near an improperly controlled smelter. These reports and photos are presented as the basis for banning all trade in wastes, even for recycling. To the contrary, these few publicized examples constitute a strong argument why the Basel Convention is so important. For example, if the plastics were truly garbage, and not recyclable raw material, the shipment should have been refused or returned under the terms of the Convention. In this way, the workers' health and the environment of the receiving country could be protected.

The Convention also covers shipments of secondary raw materials for recycling, which presents somewhat of a conundrum. The receiving country should have a proper system of environmental management to handle recycling so that the secondary materials do not present a hazard. The secondary materials are, in most cases, essential inputs to manufacturing, which creates jobs and keeps people out of poverty. The recycling can generate the wealth needed to build and maintain the environmental management system. This "chicken-or-egg" situation can be managed within the Convention. However, this is easier said than done because the Convention is not always clear. Its safeguards are clear; its definitions are muddy.

## Built-in safeguards

The principal safeguards in the Basel Convention are the requirements for prior notice and consent for shipments of covered wastes. In addition, if a waste is received, and its description has been misrepresented, the receiving country can require the originating country to take it back. If the trade is between a Party and a non-Party, the Convention requires the Party to conclude an agreement with the other country for trade in the wastes that is no less strict than the Convention. If they fail to do this, the Party is prohibited from trading.

Another important safeguard in the Convention is the requirement for "environmentally sound management" (ESM) for handling wastes. In 1989, the drafters of the Convention could not agree on what this means exactly so postponed its definition (and some other details, such as how to deal with who is liable if the management of the waste is not environmentally sound) until later. These definitions have not yet been written.

## Definitions

Besides not adequately defining ESM, the Convention does not clearly define what is a hazardous waste. It sets out categories of potentially hazardous waste or constituents in Annex I to the Convention and then lists characteristics the waste must exhibit in Annex III. If a waste is covered by being in a category of Annex I, and has a characteristic listed in Annex III, it is a hazardous waste under the Convention. Some of the categories in Annex I are:

- Clinical wastes from medical care in hospitals, medical centers, and clinics
- Wastes from the production and preparation of pharmaceutical products
- Wastes from the manufacture, formulation, and use of wood-preserving chemicals
- Wastes from the production, formulation, and use of organic solvents
- Wastes from production, formulation, and use of resins, latex, plasticizers, glues/adhesives
- Wastes from production, formulation, and use of photographic chemicals and processing materials
- Wastes from production, formulation, and use of inks, dyes, pigments, paints, lacquers, varnish

Examples of listed constituents in Annex I are beryllium and its compounds, hexavalent chromium compounds, copper compounds, zinc compounds, arsenic and its compounds, mercury and its compounds, lead and its compounds, acidic solutions or acids in solid form, asbestos, cyanides, phenols, dioxins, and furans.

The hazardous characteristics in Annex III include explosive, flammable, liable to spontaneous combustion, oxidants, poisonous, infectious, corrosive, human toxic, and ecotoxic. In addition, Annex II includes wastes "requiring special consideration," those collected from households and residues from the incineration of household wastes.

So far so good, but the system still has a lack of specificity. This is a defect that leads to defining as "hazardous" commodities that are routinely traded and recycled. Scrap metal is a good example. In 1992, the United States exported more than $1 billion worth of iron and steel scrap alone, which is recycled into "new" steel all over the world. This scrap is not considered to be a hazardous waste under U.S. law or within the OECD (Organization for Economic Cooperation and Development, whose members are the 25 most industrialized countries in the world). Under the Basel Convention, however, we would have to re-examine iron and steel scrap, comparing it to the lists and characteristics, and being concerned with the tiniest amounts of other metals and compounds, even if they are alloyed and so are not available to the environment. The Convention does not distinguish between content and availability.

Under Annex I, we would look at the list of constituents and find that, even if only in minute amounts, iron and steel scrap contains some zinc and lead and possibly their compounds. Then we would look to Annex III and would find there that the scrap is "[c]apable, by any means, after disposal, of yielding another material, *e.g.*, leachate, which possess any of the characteristics above." With no limits defined, the iron and steel scrap becomes a hazardous waste. Another example: If we are shipping 10 tons of tree bark to another country, and there is one pellet of lead shot stuck in one piece of bark, under the Basal Convention the entire shipment is "hazardous waste."

The drafters of the Convention realized that it is unlikely countries could agree on specific test methods and definitions, called "harmonization." Therefore, Annex III includes a final comment:

> The potential hazards posed by certain types of wastes are not yet fully documented; tests to define quantitatively these hazards do not exist. Further research is necessary in order to develop means to characterise potential hazards posed to man and/or the environment by these wastes. . . . Many countries have developed national tests which can be applied to materials listed in Annex I, in order to decide if these materials exhibit any of the characteristics listed in this Annex.

Countries could develop or adopt from others a national system of definitions and test methods suited to their own economies and environment. If they did, it would be a large step toward removing ambiguity. However, the Convention does not explicitly provide for mutual recognition of national systems.

A result of the definitional confusion is that something that would be hazardous waste under the Basel Convention is not necessarily a hazardous waste under a country's law. For example, many materials that are hazardous wastes under the Basel Convention are not under U.S. law, which is perhaps the strictest in the world. Without further clarification, trade in commodity-like "wastes" (raw materials for recycling) is hindered.

## Wastes for recycling

According to the Convention, the term "disposal" includes recycling operations. Hence all of the restrictions placed on trade in wastes destined for disposal apply to trade in "wastes" destined for recycling. These materials are often essential raw materials, particularly for developing countries.

In the United States, some "hazardous wastes" that are recycled or reclaimed (rather than disposed of) include solvents after they are used in industrial processes, which are then distilled (*i.e.*, recycled) so that they can be reused; certain air pollution control dusts, which can be processed to reclaim iron, zinc, lead and cadmium; and certain wastewater treatment sludges, which can be processed to reclaim metals. Not all of these classes of materials are exported. However, a great deal of other material, such as metal scraps and metal-rich manufacturing residues, is.

Developing countries use secondary raw materials (such as scraps or waste paper) because they do not have indigenous resources, or can't afford to mine them in an environmentally sound manner, or do not have the capital to build primary industries. Manufacturing based on secondary raw materials is often much less expensive. For example, primary manufacture of iron and steel involves mining iron ore and limestone, making coke from coal, and building a blast furnace to convert the ore to iron and a second furnace to convert the molten iron to steel. In secondary manufacture, scrap iron and steel are melted in one furnace to make the final product.

Many countries have found it more advantageous (economically and environmentally) to produce metals from scraps and residues that may contain 20% or more metal than from ores, which may contain as little as 0.2% metal. Obviously the amount of waste subsequently generated in such cases is vastly different.

## Trade in recyclable commodities

Trade in recyclable commodities is important to both the countries generating the recyclable materials and the countries receiving them. It is better for a generating country to export material for recycling (if they cannot do it themselves) as a form of resource conservation and environmental protection (disposal is avoided). The secondary materials benefit the importing country as a source of low-cost raw material to keep production alive and provide jobs and a source of value-added products [the value being added in the processing of the raw material into the finished product] to generate foreign exchange. This is particularly important if the importing country is a developing economy.

As an example, the United States recycles more than 150 million tons a year of industrial discards. Approximately 20 million tons of that material is exported, and a portion of the exports goes to developing countries. The Basel Convention is the safeguard to assure that the exported materials meet specifications (are not garbage), that they can be returned if misrepresented, and both importing and exporting country will work toward environmentally sound management of the plants using the secondary raw materials.

U.S. exports of recyclable materials in 1992 to developing countries were worth $2.2 billion. This included $500 million worth of just iron and steel scrap. Large customers included Argentina, Brazil, China, Guatemala, India, and South Korea.

---

*Many materials that are hazardous wastes under the Basel Convention are not under U.S. law, which is perhaps the strictest in the world.*

---

Many developing countries rely on such imports from all over the world to keep their economy going. In 1992, China imported more than 1 million tons of metal-containing secondary materials from OECD countries and only 34,000 tons from developing (non-OECD) countries. India imported almost 3 million tons of metal-containing secondary materials from OECD countries and 540,000 tons from non-OECD countries. The metals industries in these countries could not exist without participating in recycling and this "waste" trade. The same is true for trade in waste papers, which because of the ambiguities in definitions, might be classified as a Basel waste.

Some countries import more from developing than developed countries. In 1992, Pakistan imported $3,300 worth of scrap stainless steel and $52,300 worth of copper waste and scrap from developed countries and $439,300 and $1,510,000 worth respectively from developing countries. The Philippines balanced their imports of metal-containing "wastes" between developed and developing countries differently, in a ratio of two to one. Inspection of statistics from U.N. agencies shows that secondary raw materials come from and go to almost every country imaginable.

## Assuring environmentally sound management

The Convention requires assurance that exported "wastes" will be handled in an environmentally sound manner, something likely to happen in developed countries, but of great concern in developing countries. The poorer countries do not have the capital or trained people to invest in needed environmental controls.

The first attempt to define "environmentally sound management" (ESM) was to write codes of good practice for different kinds of manufacturing operations, a difficult and perhaps endless task. It is rare that plants even making the same product are operated in the same way. Another approach to ESM is to state principles of operation. One set of such principles that has been put forth includes assurance that recyclers keep adequate records accounting for all material, allow no spills, be in full compliance with local laws, properly manage residues from the processing, and that there be a government organization to regulate and enforce regulations and to assure that the plant is truly recycling by returning at least one product to commerce.

Whatever the approach, there must be adequate training of personnel. The Convention calls for such training, but it is not yet in place. Key will be training and technology transfer between suppliers (the exporters) and the processors (the importers).

## Bans on waste trade

In March 1994, at the Conference of Parties to the Basel Convention, a formal "Decision" was made by consensus (with no disagreement) that effective immediately there would be no trade in wastes for disposal between OECD countries and non-OECD countries. It was also decided by consensus (with great disagreement and controversy) that effective after 1997, there would be no trade in "wastes" for recycling between OECD and non-OECD countries. The moving force behind this Decision was the G-77 (a group of developing countries) and China. They argued that developing countries are incapable of exercising sovereignty to participate in prior notice and consent or to control imports.

It is unclear whether the G-77 countries realized the scope of the ban—that it will halt their importation of what amounts to raw materials while possibly not preventing egregious cases of actual dumping, which may go on in subversion of the Convention, with or without the ban. The ban is hypocritical. As pointed out, developing nations import Basel wastes from both OECD and non-OECD countries, and for some commodities they import far greater quantities from other developing countries than they do from the OECD. If the purpose of the ban is to prevent the importation of "hazardous wastes" into developing countries, it will thus fail miserably. It may actually do more harm than good. By excluding OECD countries from this international trade, non-OECD countries will simultaneously prevent the spread from OECD to non-OECD countries of the technology and experience required to assure ESM.

## Trade in wastes and environmental equity

The Basel Convention, and the March 1994 Decision to ban certain trade, presents conflicts in trying to reach environmental equity for developing countries. The Convention was drafted in response to the threat of widespread and egregious dumping of potentially hazardous materials in countries that do not have the controls and technology to protect human health and the environment. The Convention can succeed in this regard only if many countries are Parties and the terms of the Convention are enforced.

The Decision to ban shipments for disposal from OECD to non-OECD countries does not address trade for disposal between non-OECD countries. The G-77 denied they can exercise their sovereign powers to keep out wastes from OECD countries. But the hazard of a waste and its management do not change with its origin, so wastes from one developing country may wind up harming another developing country.

---

*Developing countries use secondary raw materials . . . because they do not have indigenous resources, or can't afford to mine them.*

---

More hurtful would be the ban on trade in "wastes" for recycling because it would deny raw materials to needed markets. This ban would avoid environmental damage (assuming no ESM) from the imported materials, but it would also deny raw materials for manufacturing. If the ban were effective and enforced, plants would close and people would lose their jobs, with effects felt within developed and developing countries, leading to a poorer environment. "Poverty is a major cause and effect of global environmental problems. It is therefore futile to attempt to deal with environmental problems without a broader perspective that encompasses the factors underlying world poverty and international inequality."[2]

Trade in recyclable commodities would continue between non-OECD countries, but there is not enough such material to keep everyone employed. For example, Thailand imports more than 70% of its iron and steel scrap from OECD countries. This much cannot be replaced by non-OECD sellers.

The most likely assurance of ESM will be from the technical training and technology transfer from OECD to non-OECD countries. However, if there is no trade, there is no incentive. ESM in non-OECD countries will suffer.

There is also the question of environmental equity in the developing countries. Without world trade, the supply of many recyclable materials will exceed demand among developed countries. Prices will fall (which will curtail recovery and recycling) and excess material will be waste for disposal. Resources will be wasted and some materials (*e.g.*, some metals) will be buried and potentially released to the environment.

So where is the equity? A ban on trade in wastes protects developing countries from environmental insult and potential harm to public health from the wastes. At the same time, a ban denies developing countries sources of raw materials, jobs, and foreign currency and capital to install and maintain ESM. What happens to the emerging economies of the former Soviet bloc? Their situation (and equity) have not been addressed in the Basel Convention.

## More unintended consequences

When the G-77 countries say they cannot exercise sovereignty to keep unwanted wastes out of their country, and want to rely on the OECD countries to do this, they seek a neo-colonialism, or perhaps an eco-colonialism. This is a step back in recognizing the rights of others.

Further, when these countries ask that exports of secondary raw materials be stopped, they are surrendering to mercantilism, something that world trade is supposed to avoid or cure. The countries are denying their people the benefits of trade and economic growth. The most rapidly emerging economies, for example the so-called "Asian tigers" like South Korea, Taiwan, and Malaysia, have built their manufacturing infrastructure around secondary raw materials.

## The other side of the coin

Critics of the trade in wastes say they are not opposed to shipments of "clean scraps." But, as pointed out in the discussion of definitions, there is no "clean scrap." Industrialized countries generate scrap in large from obsolete items, such as cars and bridges. The steel from such sources has in it, by its very nature, small amounts of materials that will classify it as a Basel waste.

These same critics, and the G-77, say that they want "clean technology." Everybody does. But all manufacturing produces some waste. The challenge is to properly manage the waste.

Finally, critics point out that if there is no place to dispose of or recycle the waste, it won't be generated. Nature does not work that way. Biological creatures (like humans) and industrial practices generate wastes because that is the nature of chemical reactions and physical processes. Not all reactions go to completion; energy cannot be completely converted into work. Certainly every practical effort should be made to minimize waste, then to recycle it, and always to properly manage it. Recycling, whether in a developed or developing country, is often the most efficient and resource conservative of methods.

The "other side of the coin" addresses the equity issues among societies by claiming to protect developing countries by denying them the resources, without addressing the balances among environmental management, public health, and poverty.

## The future situation

Sadly, the future may be more inequitable. Developing countries may choose to continue imports of secondary materials because they are essential for their well-being. They can easily do this by redefining these materials so they are not "wastes." This would subvert the Convention, and possibly lead to other subversion, maybe for disposal. All the good intentions for protecting people and the environment would be lost.

## Notes

1. In August 1992 the U.S. Senate gave their advice and consent to the United States' becoming a Party, a step that is required under the Constitution. Two years later, the United States still had not ratified the Convention (joined as a Party) because Congress must pass domestic legislation to enable enforcement of the duties under the Convention. One reason for this delay is a controversial ban in trade adopted by the Convention Parties in March 1994, which is discussed later.

2. The World Commission on Environment and Development. Gro Harlem Brundtland, Chairman. 1987. *Our Common Future*. Oxford University Press. New York. p. 3.

# Organizations to Contact

The editors have compiled the following list of organizations concerned with the issues debated in this book. The descriptions are derived from materials provided by the organizations. All have publications or information available for interested readers. The list was compiled on the date of publication of the present volume; names, addresses, and phone numbers may change. Be aware that many organizations take several weeks or longer to respond to inquiries, so allow as much time as possible.

**Agency for Toxic Substances and Disease Registry (ATSDR)**
1600 Clifton Rd. NE
Atlanta, GA 30333
(404) 452-4111

ATSDR collects, analyzes, and disseminates information on human exposure to hazardous substances, helps the Environmental Protection Agency identify hazardous waste to be regulated, and develops tests to evaluate public health risks from exposure to hazardous substances. Fact sheets, reports, and a listing of contaminated areas are available.

**Americans for Indian Opportunity (AIO)**
681 Juniper Hill Rd.
Bernalilo, NM 87004
(505) 867-0278

AIO promotes economic development for Indian tribes. It stresses that development of Indian reservations should be based on informed decision making and should be culturally, environmentally, and economically sound. AIO's publications include *You Don't Have to Be Poor to Be Indian* and *The Family Systems Report*, which touch on issues of environmental importance.

**Asian Pacific Environmental Network (APEN)**
1221 Preservation Park Way, 2nd Fl.
Oakland, CA 94612
(510) 834-8920
fax: (510) 834-8926

APEN was formed in 1993 to articulate the environmental concerns of the Asian Pacific community in the formulation of environmental policy both at the local level and within the larger environmental justice movement. Its publications include bulletins, updates, and a newsletter, which reports on issues and events in the Bay area and nationally.

**Black Workers for Justice (BWFJ)**
PO Box 1863
Rocky Mount, NC 27802
(919) 977-8162

BWFJ is a workplace-based organization fighting for the right of all workers to a safe and healthy work environment. It supports unions, elected officials, and legislation that promote environmental justice. BWFJ maintains the

Community Workers Library, and its monthly newsletter *Justice Speaks* covers workplace and environmental justice issues. Also available are videotapes documenting environmental hazards and their cleanup.

### Citizens Clearinghouse for Hazardous Waste (CCHW)
PO Box 6806
Falls Church, VA 22040
(703) 237-2249

CCHW trains and assists local people to fight for environmental justice and to build strong, locally controlled communities that are connected with others in the grassroots environmental justice movement. It conducts leadership development programs and offers training sessions on environmental issues. CCHW publishes guidebooks and fact packs, including *Pesticides in Your Community*, *Best of Organizing Toolbox*, and *Environmental Racism*. It also publishes *Everyone's Backyard*, a bimonthly magazine, and the *Environmental Health Monthly*.

### Commission for Racial Justice, United Church of Christ (CRJ)
700 Prospect Ave.
Cleveland, OH 44115
(216) 736-2160

CRJ conducts research relevant to the struggle of black and other minority communities. In 1987 it issued *Toxic Wastes and Race in the United States—A National Report on the Racial and Socio-Economic Characteristics of Communities with Hazardous Wastes*, a landmark study documenting the existence of what it termed "environmental racism." In 1994, CRJ issued an update of that report, which is available for purchase. The commission also publishes the *Civil Rights Journal*, a weekly newsletter dealing with environmental justice and other issues affecting people of color.

### Competitive Enterprise Institute (CEI)
233 Pennsylvania Ave. SE, Ste. 200
Washington, DC 20003
(202) 547-1010

CEI is a research and advocacy group supporting the establishment of a system in which the private sector, rather than the government, would be responsible for protecting the environment. It believes that by politicizing environmental issues, the environmental justice movement will encourage government regulation of business, which will then limit opportunities for minorities and the poor. CEI distributes position papers and congressional testimony. It also publishes the monthly newsletter *CEI Update* and numerous reprints and briefs.

### Council of Energy Resource Tribes (CERT)
1999 Broadway, Ste. 2600
Denver, CO 80202-5726
(303) 297-2378

CERT represents Indian tribes owning energy resources. Its mission is to support and provide technical assistance to member tribes as they develop their management capabilities and use their energy resources as a foundation for building stable, balanced, environmentally safe, and self-governed economies. Its publications include "Issues in Radioactive Waste Management in Indian Country," a briefing paper; *The Mitigation of Environmental Im-*

*pacts Due to Department of Defense Activities*, a reference manual; and the *CERT Report*, a newsletter.

**Harvard Center for Risk Analysis (HCRA)**
Harvard School of Public Health
718 Huntington Ave.
Boston, MA 02115
(617) 432-4497

HCRA's purpose is to promote reasoned public responses to a growing number of public health risks. It is developing several new methods of calculating the risk of exposure to hazardous substances and is compiling databases on the cost-effectiveness of various programs. HCRA advises legislators and presents testimony at congressional and administrative hearings. It publishes a periodic report, *Risk in Perspective*, on environmental health issues, which is available on request.

**Hudson Institute**
5395 Emerson Way
Indianapolis, IN 46226
(317) 545-1000
fax: (317) 545-1384

The Hudson Institute is a public policy research center staffed by members elected from academia, government, and industry. The institute promotes free-market principles in the solution of environmental problems. Its publications include briefing papers such as "The Organic Farming Threat to People and Wildlife," which documents the problems of reducing pesticide use; books on education and the workforce; and newsletters such as *Global Food Quarterly*, which explores issues relating to agriculture and minorities.

**National Institutes of Environmental Health Sciences (NIEHS)**
Office of Communications
PO Box 12233
Research Triangle Park, NC 27709-2233
(919) 541-3345

NIEHS, a major research organization within the National Institutes of Health, conducts and supports research to define, measure, and understand the effects of chemical, biological, and physical factors in the environment on public health. It has conducted and supported studies on the exposure effects of lead, pesticides, and other toxins. Fact sheets, research reports, and transcripts of meetings and symposiums are available.

**Native Americans for a Clean Environment (NACE)**
PO Box 1671
Tahlequah, OK 74465
(918) 458-4322
fax: (918) 452-0322

Founded in 1985, NACE's purpose is to halt the use of nuclear power, which it says has harmed the health of Native American communities involved in uranium mining and has contaminated the environment in general. Because it believes people of color bear a disproportionate burden of the environmental effects of this unsafe technology, NACE promotes renewable energy sources as an alternative to nuclear power as well as environmentally safe disposal technologies. NACE provides speakers on these and other subjects. *NACE News* is the organization's newsletter and *Raffinate* is its organizational brochure.

## People for Community Recovery (PCR)
13116 S. Ellis Ave.
Chicago, IL 60627
(312) 468-1645

PCR is a grassroots organization founded to document and fight environmental causes of health problems in local communities. One of PCR's goals is to bring African Americans into the environmental movement. The organization seeks to help local groups organize public meetings and talk to the media. PCR publishes a newsletter, *F.A.T.E.*

## Sierra Club
730 Polk St.
San Francisco, CA 94109
(415) 776-2211

The Sierra Club is an environmental conservation organization that was founded in 1892. Responding to a 1990 letter charging mainstream environmental groups of insensitivity to the environmental concerns of minority communities, it began actively to reach out to grassroots groups in their struggle for environmental justice. To address its membership profile, the organization instituted an Ethnic Diversity Task Force. The club offers brochures, position papers, and other publications. Each club chapter has its own newsletter, in addition to the national *Sierra Club Activist*. *Sierra* is the club's official magazine.

## Southwest Organizing Project (SWOP)
211 10th St. SW
Albuquerque, NM 87102
(505) 247-8832

SWOP works to empower the disenfranchised in the Southwest to realize racial and gender equality and social and economic justice. SWOP has organized nonpartisan voter registrations, candidate accountability sessions, demonstrations, petitions, marches, and other actions. SWOP's publications include *Five Hundred Years of Chicano History in Pictures*, a bilingual history book; *Intel Inside New Mexico*, a case study in environmental justice; and several pamphlets, including *Unsafe for Women, Children, and All Living Things*; *When People of Color Are an Endangered Species*; and *Toxics, Race, and Class—The Poisoning of Communities*. *Boces Unidas* is SWOP's quarterly newsletter.

## U.S. Environmental Protection Agency (EPA)
## Office of Environmental Justice (OEJ)
401 M St., SW (3103)
Washington, DC 20460
1-800-962-6215

Created by the EPA in 1992, the OEJ's purpose is to ensure that no segment of the population, regardless of race, ethnicity, culture, or income, bears a disproportionate amount of environmental pollution. OEJ coordinates with other federal agencies on environmental justice issues; provides training and technical and financial assistance to the public; and serves as a repository of papers, books, and articles on environmental justice—all of which are available to the public free of charge. OEJ also maintains the above toll-free hotline to receive calls from concerned citizens about environmental justice issues in their communities. Environmental justice coordinators, at all ten of EPA's regional offices, can offer further help or information.

**The U.S. Office of the Nuclear Waste Negotiator**
1823 Jefferson Pl. NW
Washington, DC 20036
(202) 634-6244
fax: (202) 634-6251

The office was created by the 1987 Nuclear Waste Policy Amendments Act for the purpose of working with states and Indian tribes in siting temporary storage facilities for spent nuclear fuel. In exchange for temporarily storing the waste, host states or tribes will be eligible for various benefits. The office maintains a library on these proceedings, containing media coverage, government reports, and state and tribal feasibility studies.

# Bibliography

## Books

Bunyan Bryant and Paul Mohai, eds. — *Race and the Incidence of Environmental Hazards: A Time for Discourse.* Boulder, CO: Westview Press, 1992.

Robert D. Bullard — *Dumping in Dixie: Race, Class, and Environmental Quality.* Boulder, CO: Westview Press, 1990.

Robert D. Bullard — *Unequal Protection: Environmental Justice and Communities of Color.* San Francisco: Sierra Club Books, 1994.

Robert D. Bullard, ed. — *Confronting Environmental Racism: Voice from the Grassroots.* Boston: South End Press, 1993.

Ward Churchill — *Indigenous Resistance to Genocide, Ecocide and Expropriation in Contemporary North America.* Monroe, ME: Common Courage Press, 1993.

Michael Fumento — *Science Under Siege: Balancing Technology and the Environment.* New York: Morrow, 1993.

Michael S. Greve and Fred L. Smith, eds. — *Environmental Politics: Public Costs, Private Rewards.* New York: Praeger, 1992.

Richard Hofrichter, ed. — *Toxic Struggles: The Theory and Practice of Environmental Justice.* Philadelphia: New Society, 1993.

Bryan G. Norton — *Toward Unity Among Environmentalists.* New York: Oxford University Press, 1991.

Dixy Lee Ray with Lou Guzzo — *Environmental Overkill: Whatever Happened to Common Sense?* Washington: Regnery Gateway, 1993.

Helen E. Sheehan and Richard P. Wedeen — *Toxic Circles: Environmental Hazards from the Workplace into the Community.* New Brunswick, NJ: Rutgers University Press, 1993.

United Church of Christ Commission for Racial Justice — *Toxic Wastes and Race in the United States: A National Report on the Racial and Socio-Economic Characteristics of Communities with Hazardous Waste Sites.* New York: Public Data Access: United Church of Christ, 1987.

## Periodicals

Tom Arrandale — "Environmentalism and Racism," *Governing*, February 1992. Available from Congressional Quarterly Inc., 2300 N St. SW, Ste. 760, Washington, DC 20037.

Regina Austin and Michael Schill — "Black, Brown, Red, and Poisoned," *The Humanist*, July/August 1994.

Black Workers for Justice — "Environmental Justice Now! Organize the South!" *Forward Motion*, May/June 1993. Available from the Center for Democratic Alternatives, PO Box 1884, Jamaica Plain, MA 02130.

Bill Breen — "Dueling Quotes and Other Flawed Conventions in Environmental Journalism," *Garbage*, Spring 1994. Available from Dovetail Publishers, The Blackburn Tavern, 2 Main St., Gloucester, MA 01930.

Luke W. Cole — "Remedies for Environmental Racism: A View from the Field," *Michigan Law Review*, vol. 90, no. 7, June 1992. Available from Hutchins Hall, Ann Arbor, MI 48109-1215.

Steve Coll — "Dumping on the Third World," *The Washington Post National Weekly Edition*, April 18-24, 1994.

Giovanna Di Chiro — "Defining Environmental Justice: Women's Voices and Grassroots Politics," *Socialist Review*, October/December 1992. Available from the Center for Social Research and Education, 2940 16th St., Ste. 102, San Francisco, CA 94103.

Billy Easton — "WHE ACT for Justice," *Environmental Action*, Winter 1993.

*EPA Journal* — Special Issue on Environmental Equity, March/April 1992. Available from Superintendent of Documents, GPO, Washington, DC 20402.

Karen L. Florini and Ellen K. Silbergeld — "Getting the Lead Out," *Issues in Science & Technology*, Summer 1993. Available from PO Box 661, Holmes, PA 19043.

Karl Grossman — "From Toxic Racism to Environmental Justice," *E: The Environmental Magazine*, May/June 1992. Available from Earth Action Network, PO Box 5098, Westport, CT 06881.

Juan A. Avila Hernandez — "How the Feds Push Nuclear Waste onto Indian Land," *Muckraker*, Fall 1992. Available from Center for Investigative Reporting, 530 Howard St., 2nd Fl., San Francisco, CA 94105-1200.

Steve Keeva — "A Breath of Justice," *ABA Journal*, February 1994. Available from 750 N. Lake Shore Dr., Chicago, IL 60611.

Elizabeth Martinez and Louis Head — "Media White-Out of Environmental Racism," *Extra!*, July/August 1992. Available from PO Box 911, Pearl River, NY 10965-0911.

Vernice Miller — "Self Worth and the Sewage Treatment Plant," *Christian Social Action*, May 1994. Available from 100 Maryland Ave. NE, Washington, DC 20002.

Betty Mushak — "Environmental Equity: A New Coalition for Justice," *Environmental Health Perspectives*, November 6, 1993. Available from Superintendent of Documents, Public Health Service, PO Box 371954, Pittsburgh, PA 15250-7954.

Julie A. Roque — "Environmental Equity: Reducing Risk for All Communities," *Environment*, June 1993.

Ruth Rosen — "Who Gets Polluted?" *Dissent*, Spring 1994. Available from the Foundation for the Study of Independent Social Ideas, 521 Fifth Ave., New York, NY 10017.

Michael J. Satchell      "Deadly Trade in Toxics," *U.S. News & World Report*,
                         March 7, 1994.

Michael J. Satchell      "A Whiff of Discrimination?" *U.S. News & World Report*,
                         May 4, 1992.

Valerie Taliman          "Nuking Native America," *Third Force*, March/April 1993.
                         Available from Center for Third World Organizing, 1218
                         E. 21st St., Oakland, CA 94606.

# Index